# The Counterfeit Woman

**By Dana Kramer**

**Counterfeit:**

1. made in imitation of something else with intent to deceive.

2. to make a fraudulent replica of something likely to be mistaken for something of higher value.

# TABLE OF CONTENTS

# PREFACE

The intent of this book is not to inform believers and the world of things coming upon the earth. The proclaiming of the Word through the revelation within this book is to awaken God's people. To awaken them out of the sleep of cheap grace and into the pure and holy fear of the Lord. His fear is pure and clean and is completely without darkness and evil intent. Let the fear of the Lord cause you to tremble at His Word and fill you with courage and confidence in order to stand before Him in that day!

I would like to thank my wife. I very much appreciate her support from the first days of studying this amazing book (Revelation). She never looked at me like a deer in headlights when I would share with her my findings after studying. She did contest me a few times, only because she desires to know the truth as much as I do. I thank her for the hours of listening, reading, and editing.

I would also like to thank the others that contributed hours of editing: Rebecca Bye and Joyce Ackermann. You both were a great help and I'm very appreciative to the time and work that you put into the book to edit it.

Thank you to those who helped with the cover photo: Gretchen Burkhart (photography), Jordan Ellens (make-up), Jackie Woods (model), and also to Brian & Tracy Peterson for the use of their home to take the shot. Special thanks also goes to Josiah Kramer for photo editing. You did a great job, Son.

Most of all, I want to thank the Holy Spirit for Your patience with me and speaking into my heart. Your words are very inspiring and invigorating. You have unlocked God's word so graciously and so beautifully.

--------Dana Kramer

# INTRODUCTION

I have come to the realization that from Genesis to Revelation there is a consistent theme and direction progressively moving towards an intentional result which has been revealed in the Book of Revelation. They all point to God's intended result in the end: The consummation of the ages, the eradication of evil, and the reign of Christ Jesus forevermore.

Jesus was in the beginning when God said, "*Let there be Light*" (Genesis 1:3). Jesus was not only in the bush that burned before Moses, but He was the Word that spoke to Moses. He is the Word made flesh (John 1:14). Jesus walked through the books of Isaiah, Jeremiah, Ezekiel, and all of the prophets along with the Jewish captives of Babylon (sinners just like you and me). These prophets spoke of Jesus throughout their books. Jesus experienced the horrors the Jews went through because of their own sin (Isaiah 53:3). They were despised--He was despised. They were stricken--He was stricken . . . smitten of God and afflicted. They were wounded--He was wounded and chastised. He was oppressed and cut off. It pleased the Lord to bruise Him. He was numbered with the transgressors (the Jews) and He bore the sin of many (that's us). *Now, the Lord is not slack concerning the promise of His coming . . . but is longsuffering towards us, not willing that any should perish but that all should come to repentance* (2 Peter 3:9). Jesus sits on the throne overlooking the balcony of heaven awaiting the voice of the Father who will say, "That Day has come!"

We all have different images of what "That Day" will actually look like. To some it's a day of being rescued from all sorrows. To others, it's a day of judgment upon all mankind. Still, others see it as the day which was set into motion from the very beginning when God told the serpent, "*Because you have done this, you are cursed more than every beast . . . I will put enmity between you and the woman, between your seed and her Seed . . . He shall bruise your head . . .*" (Genesis 3:15). Satan's head is bruised, but he's not in the lake of fire yet.

There is a truth in Scripture that has been lost in this age of "churchianity": The experience of trembling at His Word. This truth is proclaimed throughout all of Scripture, but is rarely experienced. Isaiah 66:2, 5 says, *"But on this one will I look:  On him who is poor and of a contrite spirit and who trembles at My Word . . . Hear the Word of the Lord, you who tremble at His Word."* Trembling at His Word only comes through intimate relationship with the One in whom we should be trembling.  No person should ever make you tremble.  Trembling before God comes from the fear of the Lord.  The fear of the Lord is full of wonder, joy, and peace. In fear and trembling, we find His rest as the writer of Hebrews proclaims:  *"Today if you will hear His voice, do not harden your hearts" . . . Let us therefore be diligent to enter that rest . . . For the Word of God is living and powerful, and sharper than any two-edged sword, piercing even to the division of soul and spirit . . . (*Hebrews 4:7, 11-12).

I must emphasize this:  If we don't read and saturate our lives in His Word (The Bible), we will very rarely hear His voice.  Jesus said an amazing thing to His disciples in the midst of proclaiming the parable of the sower (Mark 4:2-25).  They had asked Him about the parable, because they didn't understand it.  His answer was coupled with a question:  *"Do you not understand this parable? How then will you understand all the parables?"*  The understanding of this parable was crucial, since understanding the meaning of it would bring understanding to other parables.  Notice what Jesus tells His disciples right after He explains the meaning of the result of having good soil which bears fruit:  *"Is a lamp brought to be put under a basket?. . . there is nothing hidden which will not be revealed, nor has anything been kept secret but that it should come to light.  If anyone has ears to hear, let him hear.  Take heed what you hear. With the same measure [of thought and study] you give [to the truth you hear] will be the measure of [virtue and knowledge] that comes back to you--and more [beside] will be given to you who hear.  For to him who has will more be given . . . "* (Amp).  Hearing and obeying the word that is sown brings light and the diligent effort you put into understanding it will bring godly knowledge for which you will always receive more.  This brings me to what this book is all about.  In Revelation 1:1 it says, *The Revelation of Jesus Christ, which God gave Him to show His servants--things which must shortly take place.* God gave this revelation for us to know and understand. He will not give it to only one individual, but to His body (His servants). This is where the truth surrounding the parable of the sower is so important. If the soil of our heart is hard, truth will be stolen. If the soil of our heart is shallow or full of the cares of this life, truth and understanding will be lost or taken away. The Book of Revelation is a prophetic word. It could be compared to a parable since they both take a revelation in order to understand them. So, with that being said, the amount of thought and study we give to this Book will be the measure of virtue and knowledge that we will receive. Jesus sent us the Holy Spirit to reveal truth and to tell us things to come (John 16:13). It is of utmost importance for us to have good soil!

You will notice that the verse in Revelation 1:1 says, ". . . *things which must shortly take place."* These things that are proclaimed are not optional. In other words they are going to come to pass and no man can change them; not even through prayer. Prayer might delay them, but will not avert them. We must press into God so that we might have understanding on these things; otherwise, He will come as a thief--totally to our surprise. We must discern the urgency of the hour in which we live and be fearless in proclaiming the gospel. As the Lord had spoken to Isaiah, we must hear this same word: *"The Lord of hosts, Him you shall hallow, let Him be your fear, and let Him be your dread. He will be as a sanctuary"* (Isaiah 8:13-14).

I've only chosen two things from the Book of Revelation to expound upon at this time: The harlot (Great Babylon) and the beast (or beasts). I believe it is important to understand the meaning of these things so that we will be able to avoid being deceived by them. They involve a major portion of the Book of Revelation, but our focus should always be on the fact that it is the Revelation of Jesus Christ which God gave Him! All of the events point to the Main Event: Jesus coming in power and glory to deliver the kingdom to His Father. We must have God's point of view on these events. Jesus said to His disciples, *"Now learn this parable from the fig tree: When its branch has already become tender and puts forth leaves, you know that summer is near.  So you also, when you see all these things . . . know that it is near--at the door"* (Matthew 24:32-33).

That Day is swiftly coming upon us!

10

# Chapter 1
# "AND WHEN I SAW HER, I MARVELED WITH GREAT AMAZEMENT."
### Revelation 17:6

What did John see that was so amazing? Revelation 17:1-5 describes "her" as a harlot who is committing fornication and making the earth's inhabitants drunk with it. She's seen with these words written on her forehead: *MYSTERY, BABYLON THE GREAT, THE MOTHER OF HARLOTS AND OF THE ABOMINATIONS OF THE EARTH.* We have to understand that John was a very godly man and that He had walked with Jesus for three years. Also at Jesus' death he took Jesus' mother into his own home. He faced martyrdom by being boiled in oil, but was delivered from death and then sentenced to labor on Patmos. If John had seen a harlot, he would have turned away immediately just to stay pure and undefiled. If what he was looking at was indeed a harlot, why was he marveling with great amazement? Hadn't he seen harlots before? What was different about this one? Why did he marvel? Often times, when this portion of Scripture is read, it is presented as an image of a harlot dressed in provocative attire with seductive eyes; well, you get the picture. I don't believe this is what John saw.

As we look through Scripture, we can find patterns and definitions that will give us understanding to certain words and phrases. Look at Revelation 17:4 for a moment: *The woman was arrayed in purple and scarlet.* In almost every instance in Scripture when someone was dressed, or arrayed in purple, it was a sign of royalty, prominence, or high rank. In Daniel 5:7, Belshazzar (King of Babylon) was going to clothe Daniel in purple for interpreting the writing on the wall. Also, when Mordecai found favor with King Ahasuerus when a plot was discovered that Haman wanted to destroy all the Jews; Mordecai was clothed in fine linen and purple (Esther 8:15). They both were lifted to places of royalty, honor, and high rank. The Roman soldiers clothed Jesus in a purple robe mockingly proclaiming Him as King of the Jews. So the clothing that she (the harlot) wore defined her as royalty and high rank. In

Revelation 17:4, it says, *she was adorned with gold and precious stones and pearls.* We get a picture of this in Genesis 24 when Abraham called his oldest servant and sent him out to find a bride for his son, Isaac. The servant found Rebekah and adorned her with gold and said, *"My master (Abraham) made me swear to take a wife for his son from his own land".* When he found Rebekah, and adorned her with gold, he was proclaiming that she should be Isaac's wife. A bride is depicted as being adorned with jewels in Isaiah 61:10. Then later, in Ezekiel 16, the Lord proclaims Jerusalem as His bride. Verses eleven and twelve describe how the Lord adorned her with ornaments by putting bracelets on her wrists and a chain on her neck. He put a jewel in her nose, earrings in her ears, and a beautiful crown on her head. She was adorned with gold and silver. Why did the Lord do this? The answer is in verse eight of chapter sixteen: *"I swore an oath to you and entered into a covenant with you and you became Mine,"* says the Lord God. The Lord revealed His heart intention by adorning her and declaring her His bride!

So in the light of these things, John was not seeing a harlot, but a bride adorned and clothed for her husband. But, something was terribly wrong in the description. She was being described as a harlot with a golden cup in her hand, full of the filth of her fornication and the abominations of the earth. No wonder John was so amazed! Here was a bride having written on her forehead: *MYSTERY, BABYLON THE GREAT, THE MOTHER OF HARLOTS AND OF THE ABOMINATIONS OF THE EARTH.* Brides are to be single minded only for their husband. A bride is to commit her very heart and all its intimacies to her husband alone. She will not give entrance to any desire of sharing her heart with another, because she has set her affection on her husband. Her husband loves her and gives himself to her completely. This is what Paul is talking about in Ephesians 5:31, *The two shall become one flesh.*

We clearly see this harlot/bride's attitude of arrogance in Revelation 18:7. She says in her heart, *"I SIT AS QUEEN, AND AM NO WIDOW, AND WILL NOT SEE SORROW."* In other words, she's saying, "I am royalty. I am a bride. I will be rescued from any troubles." This sounds like the attitude of some believers today as they boastfully proclaim they will be raptured before any of the sorrows of the tribulation occur. I ask you, why would the Creator of the universe, who is looking intently for a bride for His Son, settle for a halfhearted one who has not been touched by any fire? Why would He take a halfhearted bride out of the world just before all hell breaks loose, when He could have a bride that has gone through it; because this bride should be like the 144,000 who follow the Lamb wherever He goes [these Jewish followers are not defiled by women, there is no deceit in them, and they are without fault before the throne of God (Revelations 14:4-5)]. If you were to choose a bride for your son, which would you choose? I will touch on the harlot's attitude again in a later chapter.

The seriousness of having this attitude (*"I sit as queen . . ."*) is revealed in the words of Jesus in Matthew 7:21-23, *"Not every one who says to Me, 'Lord, Lord', shall enter the kingdom of heaven, but he who does the will of My Father in heaven. Many will say to Me in that day, 'Lord, Lord, have we not prophesied in Your name, cast out demons in Your name, and done many wonders in Your name?' And then I will declare to them, 'I never knew you; depart from Me, you who practice lawlessness!'"* Could it possibly be that some of these people who practice lawlessness, will also be saying, *"I sit as queen, I am no widow, I will not see sorrow"*. They believe they are the bride of Christ and won't experience any sorrow, because they think they will be rescued before all the end time trials take place. The Lord did not rescue the Jews from all of their sorrows throughout their history. Only a remnant emerged alive out of Babylon and settled as God had directed them through Jeremiah (Jeremiah 29:1-7). Lawlessness is much different in definition than just being without law. It is pictured in Matthew 23:27 where Jesus speaks to the scribes and Pharisees, *"Woe to you, scribes and Pharisees, hypocrites! For you are like whitewashed tombs which indeed appear beautiful outwardly, but inside are full of dead men's bones and all uncleanness. Even so you also outwardly appear righteous to men, but inside you are full of hypocrisy and lawlessness."*

These people knew the Law, but rejected the voice of the Lord speaking to them and did what was right in their own eyes. The writer of Hebrews proclaims three times in chapters three and four, *"TODAY, IF YOU WILL HEAR HIS VOICE, DO NOT HARDEN YOUR HEARTS!"* There is an importance and emphasis on having a tender heart before the Lord to listen and obey. Since Jesus never did anything but what the Father told Him, then we should make this of utmost importance in our own lives, lest we be found lawless!

In order to understand the title, *THE MOTHER OF HARLOTS,* we must first understand the scriptural definition of the word harlot. For some clarity on this, let's look at Ezekiel 16:1-15 which describes God's love for Jerusalem:

> *The word of the Lord came to me, saying, "Son of man, cause Jerusalem to know her abominations, and say, "Thus says the Lord God to Jerusalem: Your birth and your nativity are from the land of Canaan; your father was an Amorite and your mother a Hittite. As for your nativity, on the day you were born your navel cord was not cut, nor were you washed in water to cleanse you; you were not rubbed with salt nor wrapped in swaddling cloths. No eye pitied you, to do any of these things for you, to have compassion on you; but you were thrown out into the open field, when you yourself were loathed on the day you were born. And when I passed by you and saw you struggling in your blood, I said to you in your blood, LIVE! Yes, I said to you in your blood, LIVE! I made you thrive like a plant in the field; and you grew, matured, and became very beautiful. Your breasts were formed, your hair grew, but you were naked and bare. When I passed by you again and looked upon you, indeed your time was the time of love, so I spread My wing over you and covered you nakedness. Yes, I swore an oath to you and entered into a covenant with you, and you became Mine, says the Lord God. Then I washed you in water; yes, I thoroughly washed off your blood, and I anointed you with oil. I clothed you in embroidered cloth and gave you sandals of badger skin; I clothed you with fine linen and covered you with silk. I adorned you with ornaments, put bracelets on you wrists, and a chain on you neck. And I put a jewel in your nose,*

*earrings in your ears, and a beautiful crown on your head.
Thus you were adorned with gold and silver, and your
clothing was of fine linen, silk, and embroidered cloth. You
ate pastry of fine flour, honey, and oil. You were
exceedingly beautiful, and succeeded to royalty. Your fame
went out among the nations because of your beauty, for it
was perfect through My splendor which I had bestowed on
you, says the Lord God. But you trusted in your own
beauty, played the harlot because of your fame, and poured
out your harlotry on everyone passing by who would have
it."*

From this point the word "harlot" or "harlotry" is mentioned twenty times in this chapter and the word "abominations" appears seven times. The Scriptures repeatedly demonstrate His heart for His bride and His brokenness over her harlotry of running after other lovers. She said "yes" to Him and from outward appearances she was His bride, but in her heart she began to shut Him out and find other lovers more attractive. She claimed His name, but lusted after others.

Sound familiar? I meet people who say they are believers, yet run hard after sin, as do the people of the world. Is this walking on the highway of holiness? Is this a picture of a sold out, passionate, forgiven, radically abandoned lover of Jesus? For further understanding on the definition of harlot, read Ezekiel 23; and for the term abomination, read Ezekiel chapter 8 and 18.

Proverbs 6:17-19 has a list of abominations that God hates: *A proud look, a lying tongue, hands that shed innocent blood, a heart that devises wicked plans, feet that are swift* (quick) *in running to evil, a false witness who speaks lies* (appears to know the truth and makes up lies to cover up the lack of it), *and one who sows discord among brothers.* We see through these Scriptures regarding abominations that God's definition of abomination is much different then what our definition would be. Examples: Ezekiel 18:13, . . . *has charged interest or percentage of increase on what he loaned [in supposed compassion]; shall he then live?* (Amp). He has done abomination. Notice in Proverbs 6:17-19 that a "lying tongue" is an abomination. A "false witness" is an abomination. A "proud look" (*the spirit that makes one over-estimate himself and underestimate others*—Amp) is an abomination. The "hands that shed innocent blood" are an abomination. What is our stand in regard to abortion? Wouldn't abortion be considered "innocent blood"? We cannot be neutral on this. Being neutral always errors on the side of the wicked. We must notice that the harlot is drinking from her golden cup full of abominations (Revelation 17:4)!

Just a note on the use of the Old Testament Scriptures which will be referred to many times throughout this book, Jesus and His disciples only had the Old Testament. They didn't carry a personal copy of the KJV Old Testament around to reference Scriptures any time they wanted. They had to go into the synagogue as Luke 4:16 indicates, *He came to Nazareth, where He had been brought up. And as His custom was, He went into the synagogue on the Sabbath day, and stood up to read.*

This was the custom during that time and culture, to stand up and read. When He was given the book of Isaiah, He turned immediately to chapter 61 and read it aloud. There are many other places throughout the gospels and in the letters where Jesus and the disciples referenced a Scripture, fully knowing where it was at. It makes our Bible knowledge seem like kindergarten stuff. Jesus taught from the writings of Moses, the law and the prophets, and had a very keen understanding of the Father and His mercy and grace through them. One example would be the woman caught in the very act of adultery (John 8:3-11). The law said that she should be stoned to death for this, as the scribes and Pharisees pointed out to Him. He showed much grace and mercy towards the woman by turning the focus back on the scribes and Pharisees and proclaiming, *"He who is without sin among you, let him throw a stone at her first."* They all dropped their stones and left. Jesus told her that He didn't condemn her either, but that she should stop sinning. Another example of a very emotional God extending grace and mercy is found in Isaiah 42:14-16, where God says, *"I have held My peace a long time, I have been still and restrained Myself. Now I will cry like a woman in labor, I will pant and gasp at once, I will lay waste the mountains and hills, and dry up all their vegetation . . . I will bring the blind by*

*a way they did not know; I will lead them in paths they have not known. I will make darkness light before them, and crooked places straight. These things I will do for them, and not forsake them."*
What a picture of grace. A word to men: This picture of God does, in no way, show God as weak and without strength. Some of you know what your wife was like when she was in labor; it was a very intense moment, but she didn't "lay waste" any mountains in the process. Jesus referred to the prophets on many occasions. Imagine that! The Father's love, mercy, and grace in the law and the prophets. Some seem to think that God changed His mind from judgment to mercy and grace when Jesus came to earth. God's heart of compassion was clearly seen through the prophets. Two very strategic references to the prophets are in the book of Revelation: *But in the days of the sounding of the seventh angel, when he is about to sound, the mystery of God would be finished, as He declared to His servants the prophets.* (Revelation 10:7). *And the God of the holy prophets sent His angel to show His servants the things which must shortly take place. "Behold, I am coming quickly! Blessed is he who keeps the words of the prophecy of this book,"* (Revelation 22:6).

Since He declared it to His prophets, don't you think the prophets should be studied in order to understand more clearly the Book of Revelation? The mystery of God was revealed to His prophets. And the mystery is about to be finished at the sounding of the seventh trumpet. In Luke 21:23, Jesus spoke of the prophets when He says, *"For these are days of vengeance [regarding Jerusalem], that all things which are written may be fulfilled*!" Emphasis on "all things which are written" referring to the law and the prophets. If you study Isaiah for example, you will see the words "In that day" recorded several times throughout the book, indicating a future Day of the Lord. God has given us a glimpse of the future even in the prophets. A fulfillment of Isaiah 9:6 came when Jesus was born into this world, grew, and was introduced by John the Baptist to be the Lamb of God to take away the sin of the world. Verse seven has an on going, everlasting fulfillment attached to it: *Of the (increase) of His government and peace (there will be no end).* The word increase indicates an ongoing development of these things. We will see the culmination of these things as described in

Revelation 20:14 when Death and Hades are cast into the lake of fire. Paul describes this event in 1 Corinthians 15:25-26 where he proclaims that Jesus must reign till He has put all enemies under His feet. The last enemy that will be destroyed is Death!

Going back to when Jesus read from Isaiah 61, you will notice that He stopped in the middle of a sentence. Isaiah 61:2 says, *"To proclaim the acceptable year of the Lord, and the day of vengeance of our God . . ."* He left the latter part of the verse out because it wasn't time to declare it yet. He only spoke what the Father told Him to speak. He had proclaimed that He had not come to judge the world, but that the world should be saved. In John 12:23, He speaks of the hour that has come that He should be glorified (talking of His death). He then makes an amazing statement in verse 31; *"Now the judgment (crisis) of this world is coming on [sentence is now being passed on this world]. Now the ruler (evil genius, prince) of this world shall be cast out (expelled)"* (Amp). Was the beginning of the day of vengeance and judgment starting at His death? Paraphrasing what He said: "Since My death and resurrection is soon to happen, the judgment of this world will start and Satan is going to be kicked out." The culmination of these things regarding Satan is fulfilled in Revelation12:9, when Satan is cast out of heaven and then is cast into the lake of fire in Revelation 20:10.

Jesus expounds in John 16 on the coming of the Holy Spirit: *"I still have many things to say to you, but you cannot bear them now."* The disciples were full of sorrow because He had told them that He was going away. They couldn't bear anything else at that time so He told them, *"However, when He, the Spirit of truth comes,* (after I'm gone) *He will guide you into all truth, and He will tell you things to come."* The Holy Spirit will reveal the last days via the Book of Revelation and also the law and the prophets.

Since God revealed His mysteries to the prophets, there will be many keys to unlock in their books for understanding to the Book of Revelation. Holy Spirit will reveal these mysteries and make them known to His Church as Jesus promised. We must understand that the wheat and tares are allowed to grow up together till the end, for which the wheat is harvested and the tares are burned. The harlot and the beast are allowed to develop along side His people so that there will come a defining line between the wicked and the righteous. As God used Israel's enemies such as Assyria and Babylon to purge and bring righteousness into His people, He will use the harlot and the beast to do the same in these last days. We, as His people, must completely trust the Holy Spirit to lead us through these dark times!

# Chapter 2
# "WHY DID YOU MARVEL?  I WILL TELL YOU THE MYSTERY OF THE WOMAN . . ."
Revelation 17:7

## The Woman

We see that the woman is sitting on the beast (17:3); and at the same time, she is also being carried by the beast (17:7).  This woman should be putting her trust in the Lord, but she is putting her trust in this beast and allowing the beast to carry her instead.  Some would ask, "Doesn't she see and know that this is a beast; and not of God?"  The great deceiver has done his magic and produced the appearance of an "angel of light" of the greatest magnitude, because he knows that his time is very short.  The woman, who has given herself to compromise, has been deceived because of it.  This woman who is adorned as a bride and clothed in purple, also described as the great city, is the same woman who reigns over the kings of earth (Revelation 17:18).  She is a powerful figure.  She claims she's married to her bridegroom, but notice she lives in fornication and not in adultery (which is the difference between the married and the unmarried).  God called Jerusalem an adulterous wife in Ezekiel 16:32.  He had claimed her as His own!  She was married to Him through covenant!  The harlot in Revelation is a fornicator and not in covenant with God.  She claims His name, but rejects His character and holiness.

In the past 30-40 years, we have seen a tremendous thrust in evangelism efforts to win the lost.  Many of these efforts involved only a few promises from Scripture such as "God loves you"; "He has an abundant life for you"; "Just ask forgiveness and He will give you eternal life".  These promises are true, but they do not address the utter wretchedness of man in his sin. The results were people who think they are saved from hell even though they had no change of lifestyle.  We have produced a nation of people who think they are okay with God because they live a good life. Yet, they continue living without repentance. They claim the promises, but reject His holiness, His judgments, and His discipline. In fact, I question whether they were even born again. It seems that they just became an empty shell with a "Band-Aid-Promise" labeled "God's forgiveness" yet without one ounce of change.

I am a painting contractor and work with many different types of people. I've come in contact with those who will claim to be a Christian, for which I rejoice, but then discover their life is far from looking like Jesus. Yes, I'm aware of those who desire to become like Him yet slip, trip, stumble and fall; then turn around, confess their sins and repent. They accept His forgiveness with a turning; with a change of heart.

I know change is sometimes a difficult thing for people. My life was broken on drugs and when I met the Lord I struggled for several months going back into it and then repenting. After falling many times and knowing I was purposely doing it, I came to a face to face decision with God one night. I was coming back from a friends house after getting very high and I turned to see a lit Shell gas station sign that had the "S" burned out. At that moment God spoke to me and said, "If you don't repent of doing drugs you're going to go to Hell." Needless to say it rocked my world. I made a commitment to the Lord to never do drugs again. However, I was tempted again on a trip that I had made to the state of Washington, in which a friend of mine and I spent three weeks visiting his parent's house in Tacoma. His brother and his girlfriend were pot smokers and said that we could partake anytime that we wanted. We didn't have to ask. Well, being so far away from home and out in the Washington forest you can imagine what went through my brain. I walked into their trailer one day when no one was around and there on the table was the biggest bag of pot I had ever seen. I stood there--like a deer in headlights--for what seemed to be an eternity. Then the Holy Spirit said in a very loud voice, "RUN!" I turned to go out of the trailer and ran as fast and as far away as my legs would take me. I've been free since that day. My struggles have been matched with my "yes" to the Lord. If I had given into temptation I would have been enslaved and probably even tried to justify it. Yes,

I know that change is hard, yet what I'm starting to see more frequently is the acceptance and embracing of the things of this world all the while claiming God's grace over their life so they can get close to the world without getting burned. Another way this appears is when someone is being tempted to sin and then willfully makes the decision to do so, because they know they can ask forgiveness (of a merciful, gracious Savior who forgives) with no regret. In this response, there is very little sincere love for the Lord, because Jesus said, "*If you love Me, keep My commandments*" (John 14:15). One of these commandments being, *Do not love the world or the things of the world* (1 John 2:15).

A few years ago I was working with a painter who claimed to be a believer. We were both subcontracting for another company and working in the same house. I overheard an exchange he had with a person who was delivering paint to him. He proceeded to rebuke this delivery guy for something that was wrong with the order, using several cuss words and expletives. This was done in the presence of other workers at the house. No more than ten minutes later, he began trying to give a witness to the other workers about Jesus. Sadly, they wanted no part of what this guy had and their response was, "Shut up and don't talk to us about God!" This wasn't just a slip up on his part; it was his way of life. Another example is when my wife and I started attending a church close to where we lived. At first we enjoyed the services and the preaching. People did accept Jesus on some occasions and there was a serving attitude with a focus to win the lost. But as time went on we began to see many compromises among the people that were leaders in the church. On many occasions, the youth worship leader would wear a "Led Zepplin" T-shirt while leading the youth in worship. Jimmy Page (lead singer and songwriter of Led Zepplin) is known for his involvement in the occult and his purchase of occultist Aleister Crowleys haunted mansion.[1] Even if there wasn't an awareness of these things, the lyrics to the songs would be enough to eventually convict a lover of Jesus to forsake this music. On other occasions,

---

[1] Links to web sites that had additional information regarding these statements:
www.cuttingedge.org/News/n2003-1.cfm
en.wikipedia.org/wiki/Jimmy_Page

he would wear a "Bourbon Street" (French quarter) T-shirt while leading worship. I could give a web address, but the addresses given do not convey the actual reality of what it's like being on Bourbon Street in the French Quarter. Nudity, perversion, and lust make up a majority of the businesses on this street. Even if you have never set foot on Bourbon Street, the partying and drunkenness should indicate what it's like. Would this be considered a dichotomy? Yes! What is being taught to new believers? Does the secular have anything to do with the holy? Does light have fellowship with darkness? I had also joined the worship team at this church during our time there and began discovering that the main service worship leader and other singers and musicians on the team were very much steeped in secular rock and roll and frequented many of the concerts held in the surrounding area, raving about how great they were. Dichotomy? Yes! What are they teaching new believers? In all these things they were endeavoring to get those who were unsaved into the church, but wanted to make them feel comfortable by presenting the secular and endeavoring to use it to get them saved. But I ask you, what would they be saved from, since the secular was accepted, along with drinking and frequenting bars and worldly concerts just for enjoyment under the guise of "Christian fellowship"? We are seeing the fulfillment of Isaiah 5:20, *"Woe to those who call evil good and good evil; who put darkness for light, and light for darkness; who put bitter for sweet, and sweet for bitter!"* The Church is loosing discernment and muddying the lines between the holy and the profane.

A most recent example of this lack of discernment was when the "gay marriage" bill was being voted on here in Minnesota. It was reported that there were several pastors who supported this bill. So, in wanting to become like the world, in order to win a lost world to Jesus, there has come the heart of a harlot. She has sold herself to other lovers, and not to God! To go one step further; to teach, either by speech or through example, that living like the world is acceptable to God in order to win the world, is the very essence of the "Mother of Harlots".

In Romans 11:11, Paul proclaims a mystery: God opened up salvation to the Gentiles because of grace and also to provoke Israel to jealousy through lavishing His favor upon the Gentiles in order that Israel would come to Him. If we live as a harlot, how will our life with Jesus be attractive to the Jews? If a God-fearing Jew (who did not know Jesus) knew from the Torah what was pleasing to God, came and visited some of these churches and met some of these people who claim Jesus, would they decide Jesus was indeed the Messiah? Would the church's lifestyle be provoking enough for Jews to believe? If we don't look like Jesus, how will the Jews become jealous of what we have? It's no wonder there is a tremendous lack of power in the Church today.

Throughout Jesus' teachings, He commands us to be holy. He says, *"No one can serve two masters . . . If you love Me then keep My commandments . . . Enter through the narrow gate . . . If anyone causes one of these little ones, who believe in Me to stumble, it would be better for him if a millstone were hung around his neck, and he were thrown into the sea,"* (Luke 16:13, John 14:5, Mark 9:42). These people that Jesus just spoke of would be no different than Judas Iscariot. Jesus said it would have been good if Judas had not been born. We, as God's people, are so prone to want to get by with as little as possible, yet get as much as we can. Salvation is free, but it costs us everything! Jesus also said another amazing thing; *"Blessed are the pure in heart* (undefiled by the world), *for they shall see God!"* Let's not be caught in harlotry when He returns. If these who are stumbling blocks continue in their compromises, they will certainly be deceived by this so called "false Christ" that is to come! They will not see God in the land of the living!

## "The Seven Heads Are Seven Mountains On Which the Woman Sits . . ." Revelation 17:9

## What is a mountain?

The woman is sitting on seven mountains. There is a widely known teaching that the seven mountains are the seven hills that the

Vatican sits on in Rome. Before we make any conclusions on whether this is true, we must have scriptural understanding of what a mountain is. According to Scriptures that mention the word mountain, we see that in most cases a mountain is not a massive rock structure that men find so exciting to climb. A mountain is actually something that we are to change, destroy, uproot, make low, hide in, cast into the sea, or get revelation on. Here are some scriptures that talk about mountains (all emphasis added is mine):

Luke 4:5-6: *Then the devil, **taking Him up on a high mountain**, showed Him all the kingdoms of this world in a moment of time. And the devil said to Him, "All this authority I will give you, and their glory; for this has been delivered to me, and I give it to whomever I wish."* This would be impossible in the natural, because no one could see all the kingdoms of this world in a moment of time unless given a revelation of it. This mountain is Satan's belief system and he revealed it to the Son of God. Notice he says, *"All this authority has been delivered to me and I can give it to whomever I wish."* His mountain, first established in the garden with Adam and Eve, has been increasingly growing throughout the history of man because man has continually been deceived by him. Man continues to fall into Satan's trap. Leaders and rulers of peoples and nations continue to fall into this deception. Many actors, musicians and writers are also deceived by his mountain so they give into evil spirits that speak to them telling them they will be great and famous if they allow them entrance into their lives. The lust for fame and greatness is once again accommodated by the master of deception. God looks for those who are completely His so that He can strongly support them. Where are the Elijah's of God that live in His holy mountain?

Malachi 1:2-3: *"I have loved you," says the Lord. Yet you say, "In what way have you loved us? Was not Esau Jacob's brother?" says the Lord. "Yet Jacob I have loved; but Esau I have hated, and **laid waste his mountains** and his heritage."* From the very beginning Esau was rejected. As Jacob and Esau grew up, it became more evident that Gods hand was on Jacob, but completely against Esau. Jacob received the blessing. Esau became a rebellious servant because he despised his birthright. Therein lays his belief system. He saw his birthright as unimportant and lived his life

26

according to his fleshly desires.  He married two women who were Hittites and they became a grief of mind to Isaac and Rebekah (Genesis 26:35).  Esau's decisions caused him to become bitter towards Jacob.  This bitterness was passed on from generation to generation.  The prophets talk much about Edom (Esau's descendants).  It doesn't end up well for Edom.

Isaiah 40:4:  "*Every **mountain** and hill brought low.*"  Spoken by John the Baptist concerning what would happen because of the appearance of the Messiah.  Every lofty thing, every man-made kingdom that rises up against the knowledge of God will be brought low.

Isaiah 41:15:  "*Behold, I will make you (Israel) into a new threshing sledge with sharp teeth; you shall **thresh the mountains** and beat them small.*"  Have you ever seen a threshing machine driving over a mountain and doing this?  This can't possibly be talking about actual mountains.  It has to be a belief system of some kind, or a life's paradigm.  God is going to use Israel, in the end, to radically change national mindsets into God's mindset.

Zechariah 8:3:  *Thus says the Lord, "I will return to Zion, and dwell in the midst of Jerusalem [His Kingdom], Jerusalem shall be called the City of truth, the **mountain of the Lord** of hosts, the **Holy Mountain.**"*  Jerusalem is the Mountain of the Lord!  Revelation chapters 21 and 22 talk of this Holy Mountain which is described as the New Jerusalem.

Revelation 6:15:  *And the Kings of the earth, the great men, the rich men, the commanders, the mighty men, every slave and free man hid themselves in the caves and the rocks of the **mountains,** and said to the **mountains** and rocks, "fall on us and hide us from the face of Him who sits on the throne and from the wrath of the Lamb! For the great day of His wrath has come and who is able to stand?"*

Isaiah 2:17-19:  . . . *In that day . . . they shall go into the holes of the rocks, and into the caves of the earth, from the terror of the Lord and the glory of His majesty, when He arises to shake the earth mightily.*

Those mentioned in Revelation 6:15 all wanted their belief system to cover and hide them from His face. All these had belief systems outside of God. Belief systems of power; where man can have all the authority over man that he desires. Belief systems of pleasure--the world is full of pleasurable experiences today. The belief system of money and fame--money is sought after most aggressively and is believed to be the answer to all things. Finally, there is the belief system of "Me". "I" am the most important individual on the planet. "I" am the only person who can make me happy. "I" make my own way in this world because nobody else can do it like "I" do. All these are mindsets that have been sought after and developed over a life span. They are seeking to cover themselves with these; as if they are considered by God as legitimate coverings. Also, there is another belief system rising today in this world in regard to Islam and Allah, for which I will address in chapter six.

Notice also in Revelation 6:15 they wanted the . . . *rocks to hide them.* What is a rock according to Scripture? Psalm 61:2 states, *Lead me to the **rock** that is higher than I. He only is my **Rock** and my salvation, the **rock** of my strength,* (Psalm 62:2,6,&7). *"And on this **rock** I will build My church, and the gates of hell shall not prevail against it,"* (Matthew 16:18). This was what Jesus said of Peter's revelation of Himself being the Christ, the Son of the Living God! Deuteronomy 32:18, *"Of the **Rock** who begot you, you are not mindful, and have for gotten the God who fathered you."* It is only on 'this Rock' that we are fathered by God. So we see that a "rock" is a revelation; a confession, of the God/god that we hold on to. This "rock" that Jesus mentioned, will stand against the gates of hell. We can hide in this rock. We cannot hide in the rock we have created, nor can we hide in the mountain of our belief system.

## "Here Is Wisdom . . ." Revelation 17:9

In Revelation 13:1, it says that on the beast's seven heads there is a blasphemous name. These heads are proclaiming divine status; usurping the place and title that only the Lord God Himself can claim. Again in Revelation 17:9-11, there are seven heads on this beast. There are also seven kings mentioned, of which five have fallen, one is, and the other has not yet come. The beast is the eighth (king) and is of the seven.

What I'm about to say, concerning the five kings that have fallen, could be in question, but it seems to make sense. Since this harlot has on her forehead the words, *"Babylon the great,"* we must take into consideration that there is a connection with Babylon of the Old Testament. Babylon was used by God to discipline Israel. Babylon knew that God was using them to discipline Israel. We see this in Jeremiah 40:1-3; Babylon's captain of the guard took those in Jerusalem and Judah away, captive in chains to Babylon. The captain of the guard said these words to Jeremiah, *"The Lord your God has pronounced this doom on this place. Now the Lord has brought it, and has done just as He said. Because you people have sinned against the Lord, and not obeyed His voice, therefore this thing has come upon you."* God used Babylon (a heathen nation) to bring correction and discipline to Israel because of their backsliding. God will use a donkey as He did with Balaam to try to get our attention if we have gone astray. What people, situations, or even possible "donkeys" has God used in your life to get your attention? What foreign nation(s) will God use against America as He did with Israel?

There is one book that stands out on this subject of five fallen kings. The book of Daniel in chapter 2 could be a key to partially unlocking this mystery. Nebuchadnezzar had a dream of an image. *"The images head was fine gold, its chest and arms of silver, its belly and thighs of bronze, its legs of iron, its feet partly of iron and partly of clay. A stone, cut out without hands, struck the image. The iron, the clay, the bronze, the silver, and the gold were crushed together and became like chaff . . . so no trace was found. The stone that struck the image became a great mountain and filled the whole earth"* (Daniel 2:34-35).

Daniel's interpretation of these things is in verse 44 of chapter 2: *"And in the days of these kings the God of heaven will set up a kingdom which shall never be destroyed; and the kingdom shall not be left to other people; it shall break in pieces and consume all these kingdoms, and it shall stand forever."* I see five kingdoms, of which the last is being mixed with fragile clay. All five of these kingdoms have fallen and have been completely broken in pieces and consumed by God's kingdom. God used each one of these wicked kingdoms to establish His Kingdom in His remnant. Jesus came forth during the last kingdom (Rome) and carried His Kingdom from that point on. Each one of these wicked kingdoms had one desire: to rule and dominate the entire world! They were given over to much pleasure and wealth. Each of these ruling kingdoms have been completely broken in pieces and crushed.

There is one ruling right at this present time who dominates the world (Revelation 17:10). Could it be that this one is Satan himself or could it be that there is one nation that is ruling over the rulers of the entire earth? Isaiah equates the king of Babylon with Lucifer in Isaiah 14:4, 12-13. In these Scriptures, he addresses the King of Babylon (verse 4) and continues with a proverb against this King (verse 12) where he addresses Lucifer's attitude in this King. *"For you* (Lucifer) *have said in your heart: 'I will ascend into heaven, I will exalt my throne above the stars of God . . . I will be like the Most High.'"* The king of Babylon had the same heart as Lucifer. I know what it says about Nebuchadnezzar in Daniel 4:28-37, concerning his change of heart, but he was still the head of gold and was completely crushed by the Stone that became a mountain and filled the earth. He had this dream of the image in the second year of his reign. Shortly afterwards, he made a golden image and was extremely enraged because three Hebrews wouldn't bow down and worship it. This serves as an example for us today and is a shadow of things to come.

Jeremiah 25:12 says, *"Then it will come to pass, when seventy years are completed, that I will punish the king of Babylon and that nation, the land of the Chaldeans, for their iniquity" says the Lord.* I have carried the idea that Nebuchadnezzar could have repented and become a godly king but Scripture seems to indicate that Babylon was a wicked nation and God was going to judge it. Notice what Isaiah says in chapter 47:5-11 (emphasis mine) concerning the Chaldeans of Babylon: *"Sit in silence, and go into darkness, O daughter of the Chaldeans; for you shall no longer be called the **Lady of Kingdoms**. I was angry with My people; and profaned My inheritance* (Judah), *and given them into your hand* (Babylon). *You showed them no mercy . . . and you said, **'I shall be a lady forever.'** Therefore hear this now, you who are given to pleasures . . . who say in your heart, 'I am, and there is no one else besides me; I shall not sit as a widow, nor shall I know the loss of children'; but these two things shall come to you in a moment, in one day; the loss of children, and widowhood. They shall come upon you in their fullness because of the multitude of your sorceries . . . for you have trusted in your wickedness; you have said, 'No one sees me'!*

This portrayal of ancient Babylon, Isaiah proclaims can be compared to the explanation concerning "Great Babylon" in Revelation 18:7: *She says in her heart, "I sit as queen, and am no widow, and will not see sorrow." Therefore her plagues will come in one day . . . for by your sorcery all the nations were deceived.* God revealed His purposes through His prophets and His purposes will be carried through perfectly as the end times unfold!

One Scripture on the woman from chapter 17 states, *I saw her drunk with the blood of the saints and with the blood of the martyrs of Jesus.* What could this mean but that she was overjoyed that they were taken out. Why? The saints and those who are willing to die for Jesus will endeavor to live like Jesus. They have the Holy Spirit on their lives and the truth of God's word in their hearts. This is a direct threat to those who walk in compromise. When someone has compromised in their heart, anyone who represents light and truth brings a direct confrontation to their darkness. We see this happen with Jesus and the scribes and Pharisees many times in Scripture. When Pilot presented Jesus before the people, they became "drunk" with His blood and stirred the Jews into one unified cry, "Crucify Him!" All they could see was Jesus crucified. They had rejected Him as being the Messiah and had reduced Him to just a man. The Mother of Harlots will be drunk on the blood of the saints and the martyrs of Jesus in exactly the same way. She will reject these whom God will use to bring conviction upon her wayward soul.

# Chapter 3
# "WHY DID YOU MARVEL? I WILL TELL YOU THE MYSTERY OF . . .
# THE BEAST THAT CARRIES HER, WHICH HAS SEVEN HEADS AND TEN HORNS."
Revelation 17:7

## The Beast

The Apostle Paul talks about this beast in his letter to the Thessalonians. *That Day* (the coming of Jesus*) will not come, unless the falling away comes first, and the* **man of sin** *is revealed, the son of perdition who opposes and exalts himself above all that is called God or that is worshiped, so that he sits in the temple of God, showing himself that he is God. The coming of the* **lawless** *one is according to the working of Satan, with all power, signs and lying wonders and with all unrighteous deception among those who perish, because they did not receive the love of the truth, that they might be saved, and for this reason God will send them strong delusion, that they should believe the lie,* (2 Thessalonians 2:3-4, 9-11). The falling away and the man of sin go hand in glove. The falling away is because the man of sin is revealed which causes them to go into strong delusion and then they believe the lie that has been presented to them by Satan.

Paul says the mystery of lawlessness is already at work. As I have mentioned in the first chapter of this book; lawlessness is not just being without law; it is the rejection of God's voice speaking into our lives. This "lawlessness" will continue to be on the increase and the restrainer (2 Thessalonians 2:7) will be taken out of the way when it has reached its fullest measure. Then the lawless one will be revealed as it says in 2 Thessalonians 2:8. Jesus touches on this lawlessness in Matthew 24:12-13, *"Because lawlessness will abound, the love of many will grow cold. But he who endures to the end shall be saved."* This love, Jesus talks of, is not just brother to

34

brother or for people, it is directly related to our love for God and His Holiness. To love God is to obey Him and embrace His Holiness. To ignore God's voice and His Holiness is lawlessness. Could it be that the present day emphasis of grace only (opposed to the fear of the Lord) is making God into a soft, sugar daddy kind of God? One who blinks at our sin and says, "Oh that's ok. You are not perfect." So we don't really listen when God speaks and then we turn a deaf ear to what He proclaims is holy. God is love (1 John 4:8), but He is also jealous over us. If we don't correctly perceive His love, we will stray from it. We then become a law unto ourselves by what we approve of or don't approve of in Scripture. This is lawlessness. The ever increasing lawlessness that we see today is bringing forth the pregnancy and delivery of the very **man of lawlessness** that Paul describes. Remember, *He who endures to the end shall be saved.* Or paraphrasing: 'He who loves God and His voice firmly until the end and does not give into compromise shall be saved'.

Paul talks of **one beast** (the lawless one) in 2 Thessalonians 2. Revelation 13 talks of **two beasts**: one from the sea and the other from the earth. Both Paul and Jesus mention Satan being directly behind this beast. Paul said, *The coming of the lawless one is according to the working of Satan, with all power, signs, and lying wonders* (2 Thessalonians 2:9). And Jesus said in Revelation 13:2, *The dragon gave him his power, his throne and great authority.* This beast is a direct manifestation of the working of Satan with deception. Notice what it says about the beast in Revelation 17:8. It says twice in this verse: *He was, and is not, and yet is, and will ascend out of the bottomless pit.* This is the Lord's description of the beast. The Lord also establishes a description of Himself in Revelation 1:8 and 16:5, *He who is and who was and who is to come, the Almighty.* What a direct contrast! Again, Satan portrays himself as God through this beast and endeavors to deceive, through satanic power, anyone he can into worshiping this beast. The mention of the second beast in Revelation 13:11 (emphasis mine), says that *he exercises all the authority of the first beast **in his presence**.* Don't you find this an unusual statement? Another unusual statement in 13:14 (emphasis mine), says *he deceives those who dwell on the earth by those signs which he was granted to do **in*** *the sight of the beast.* Again in 13:5 (emphasis mine), *He was given a mouth*, which refers to the first beast. What are we to conclude of these things? He's "given a mouth", as if he didn't already have one? The second beast works "in the presence" of the first beast and also performs signs "in the sight of the beast". It sounds like this beast is not a man, but a spirit being . This spirit being is proclaimed as "god" by his people. This "god" speaks to people and has a prophetic voice through his own prophets just as our God and Father does. As we established earlier, the woman adorned with gold and jewels thinks she is a bride. It says in Revelation 17:8, that they will marvel when they see the beast. I must ask, "Do they think they are seeing the return of Jesus Christ? Jesus warned His disciples and us to not be deceived. He said, ". . . *then if anyone says to you, 'Look, here is the Christ!' do not believe it.*" (Matthew 24:23). Jesus will come as the lightning that flashes from east to west.

As we look at the second beast or the false prophet, the name given to him in Revelation 19:20, we can compare this activity to the activity of Jesus when He walked the earth. God (was given a mouth) through Jesus and Jesus Himself exercised the authority of His Father (in His Fathers presence) and performed signs (in the sight of His Father). All of this beast's activity is through the working of Satan in order to deceive mankind. This false prophet continues with deception through lying signs and wonders. He proceeds by telling man to make an image to the beast. Power was given so that this image could speak and put to death those who don't worship it. The images or idols that man created throughout history did not speak. In fact Isaiah presents the foolishness of man in Isaiah 44 where he portrays man as burning half of his idol in fire to warm himself and then falls down in front of the rest of it to worship it. Psalm 115:4-5 speaks of these idols as having mouths but not being able to speak. The illusive power of Satan will manifest itself with great deception and many will be deceived.

I used to believe that I was so in tune with God that I would be able to spot this impostor the moment that I saw him. But I was forgetting all that is going to happen on this earth by way of judgments and the tremendous increase of darkness through raw satanic power and the great multitude of those who have given

36

themselves to this power, I began to realize the utter desperation and deception that will be upon the people of this earth and sensed the Lord calling me to give myself continuously to His Word and to seek His face. As Hebrews 5:14 says, *Solid food* (not milk) *belongs to those who are of full age, that is, those who by reason of use (or trained by practice have their senses exercised to discern both good and evil* (Amp). If we don't know His word and are not trained by it, we will not have discernment. It's the one who seeks God through His Word in the secret place and continues to gaze at Jesus that will stand in these last days.

The things that are coming upon this earth will cause many to be offended at God and His people. One of the latest international occurrences of being offended at God's people was demonstrated through the situation with the ousting of the Muslim Brotherhood's president of Egypt. If you have followed these events, the Muslim Brotherhood was offended by the Christians in Egypt and began to kill them and burn down their churches. They blamed Christians for the fall of their president Mohamed Morsi, a member of the Muslim Brotherhood. The persecution and killing of believers since then has been steadily on the rise in many nations. Since then, ISIS (now known as IS--Islamic State) has risen in Iraq and has taken over many cities giving the Christians in those cities a mandate: either convert to Islam or die. Christians are fleeing for their lives. This could cause offense in some believers wondering why God does not intervene.

Similarly, we as believers are also vulnerable and could be offended at God when we see the last days events unfold before our very eyes. One such event was the earthquake and tsunami that happened in Japan on March 11, 2011.[2] There were more than 28,000 people left dead or missing. This event was probably a major source of offence to some people. I remember the response of a friend of mine back in 1971 after I had gotten saved. I had told him of my conversion and acceptance of Jesus, so he proceeded to read the Bible for himself. He came to the place in Joshua 6:21 where the

---

[2] Thought provoking video on what happened to Japan:
Nationalgeographic.com/video/news/japan-tsunami-2011-vin

Israelites utterly destroyed all that was in the city (man, woman, young and old, ox, sheep and donkeys) with the edge of the sword. Needless to say he was offended by this and said, "If God is behind that event then I want nothing to do with Him." I'm glad to say he got over his offence and is still serving God today. Satan is the devious master schemer behind all offenses. Remember what Satan tried to do to Job in Job 1-2. He tried to get Job to pick up an offense toward God, but Job remained faithful. Being offended would no doubt cause us to look for a more appealing answer to our dilemma. Satan knows this very well. Notice the number of those offended is increasing in the United States as well. The Ten Commandments are being taken out of government buildings; manger scenes and crosses are being removed because they might offend another religion. And some religions become offended very easily. You can't even say "Merry Christmas" in some places. So what does all this mean? The pressure is mounting, leading up to and culminating the great falling away and turning to the man of sin; or as Jesus puts it, the beast, and the abomination of desolation.

Jesus explained to the scribes and Pharisees in Matthew 23:37-24:1 (emphasis mine) saying, "*O Jerusalem, Jerusalem, the one who kills the prophets and stones those who are sent to her! How often I wanted to gather your children together, as a hen gathers her chicks under her wings, but you were not willing! See! Your house is left to you* **desolate . . .**"

Jesus said their temple is left "desolate" just before He left the building! It has been desolate since then and still would be if it were to be rebuilt today. The "abomination" or "image" spoken of (which will be standing in the holy place) has many preludes to it. One of which is expounded on in Ezekiel 8:3-6. It says (emphasis mine), *He stretched out the form of a hand, and took me by a lock of my hair; and the Spirit lifted me up between earth and heaven, and brought me in visions of God to Jerusalem, to the door of the north gate of the inner court, where the seat of the* **image** *of jealousy was, which provokes to jealousy . . . so I lifted my eyes toward the north, and there...was this* **image** *of jealousy in the entrance. Further more He said to me, "Son of man, do you see what they are dong, the great* **abominations** *that the house of Israel commits here."*

38

The image of jealousy is directly related to the word abomination. **They commit abomination with the image of jealousy!** God becomes jealous when man creates an image that replaces adoration towards Him. He calls it an abomination. Thus we have an image of jealousy. So when it is spoken concerning the **abomination of desolation**; this image fills up the desolation that Jesus spoke of in Matthew 23:38 (emphasis mine) *"See! Your house* (temple) *is left to you* **desolate***, for I say to you, you shall see Me no more until . . . "* This abomination proclaims himself as God and fills up the desolation that was left when Jesus left the temple. This beast/image abomination presents himself as an angel of light, transformed by Satan himself. Satan has the ability to make himself look so beautiful. If this wasn't true he would not be able to deceive anyone. One day we will see him as he is in all of his hideousness and his life sucking traits will be exposed for all to see. Notice the end coming to this angel of light and his kingdom which is written in the fifth bowl judgment (Revelation 16:10): *The angel poured out his bowl on the throne of the beast, and his kingdom became full of darkness; and they gnawed their tongues because of the pain.* I'm reminded of a quote from Jesus in Matthew 6:23 which says, *" If the light that is in you is darkness, how great is that darkness!"* If what you believe in is actually rooted in darkness, yet you live in that belief as if it were light, that darkness becomes greater with an intensely stronger bondage. It was revealed to the beast worshipers that the light they thought the beast was bringing was actually darkness and not light. This revelation brought great pain of body, soul, and spirit.


## The Mystery of the Beast

> *"The ten horns which you saw are ten kings who have*
> *received no kingdom as yet, but they receive authority*
> *for one hour as kings with the beast. These are of one*
> *mind, and they will give their power and authority to the*
> *beast. These will make war with the Lamb, and the*
> *Lamb will overcome them . . . "* (Revelation 17:12-14).

*"The ten horns which you saw on the beast, these will
hate the harlot, make her desolate and naked, eat her
flesh and burn her with fire. For God has put it into
their hearts to fulfill His purpose, to be of one mind, and
to give their kingdom to the beast, until the words of
God are fulfilled,"* (Revelation 17:16-17).

These ten kings are beast worshipers. They believe in the
beast and they obey all that the beast says to them. The beast's
words are not just spoken words, but will also be recorded words for
he has also documented his word for his followers. As in
Christianity, God has given His word to us, speaking to us directly in
our spirit, and also through His written Word, the Bible. Some
simply take His Word, believe it and then go out and do exploits in
His name. Others hear His Word, but are distracted by other things
and would be called lukewarm, moderate, dull, and asleep. We see
this same thing happening concerning the beast and his followers.
Some are very radical and others are distracted and asleep. So we
see this trend in Christianity and so it is with those who follow the
beast. Some don't worship the beast or live out his word. Revelation
13:15 mentions this beast/image as being able to speak and those
who don't worship will be killed. These would be called moderate or
unbelievers. They don't listen to what the beast is speaking. Since
all are required to worship this beast and his image, if they don't,
they will be killed. Most likely an action carried out by those who
are radical in their loyalty to the beast.

Notice these ten kings have no kingdom, yet are of one mind,
intent, and/or purpose. These kings are hell bent to see the beast
come into power. And, they have no real nation or country to rule
over. They are rogue kings until the beast comes into power, they
will reign with him *for one hour*. This could be a literal hour or a
short time period (maybe three and one half years). Again, their
motivation is to make sure the beast comes into power. Remember,
they do not just believe and give their kingdom to the beast; they are
ultimately believing and following Satan himself; taking on his very
character. Satan is described as a deceiver, liar, thief, murderer, and
blasphemer. As we have seen before, Paul describes him in 2
Corinthians 11:14 as transforming himself into an angel of light. So,

what should we be looking for in regard to these things? Is this beast a transformation of Satan to look like an angel of light? He is called "God" by his followers? (Which, by the way, is blasphemy) I ask you to consider how many different terrorist groups are rising up today? They all seem to have the same mandate. They have no real kingdom, but are only cell groups. Even though they differ, they are all of the same mindset: destroy Israel and spread Islam.

The book of Daniel brings out two very important points on this topic. First point: Daniel 7, had a vision of a beast with ten horns. Among these ten horns a little horn came up which had eyes like a man, and a mouth that spoke pompous words (or blasphemy). This little horn was making war against the saints (7:21-22), and prevailing against them **until**, the Ancient of Days came and a judgment was made in favor of the saints of the Most High. Revelation 17:14 also speaks of the ten horns who are actually ten kings, and they will make war with the Lamb, and the Lamb will overcome them. God's message to us in all of this is that He is very much in control and cannot be overcome. He comes out most victorious!

The second point is found in verse twenty-five of Daniel, Chapter 7, which reads, *He shall speak pompous words against the Most High, shall persecute the saints of the Most High and shall intend to change times and law.* If we are observant today, we will see this very thing happening right before our eyes! It has been like "a frog in the kettle" experience since 9/11 happened. Ever so slowly, yet very methodically, laws around the world are being changed. Yes, it is happening in America. Sharia Law is infiltrating and being implemented throughout the world today.

Just a thought on the word "little"; Daniel 7:24 speaks of a *little horn who will persecute the saints and change times and law . . . for a time and times and half a time* (a three and one half year period). Revelation chapters 11-13 also describe the events that will happen for a three and one half year period. I would like to point out that the angel described in Chapter 10, who precedes these events in chapters 11-13, prophesies by his very appearance and description that these events are written in a "little" book open in his hand (verse

41

2). He proceeds to set his right foot on the **sea** and his left foot on the **earth** and cries out with a LOUD VOICE, as when a lion roars. He's prophesying by his very presence and the position of his feet. You will notice in Revelation 13 that the first beast comes out of the *sea*. The second beast comes out of the *earth*. What does this proclaim, but what Paul says in 1 Corinthians 15:25, *He* (Jesus) *must reign till He has put all enemies under His feet!* The angel has his foot on the sea and earth representing that *all* enemies are under His feet. This prophetic gesture indicates the beast out of the sea and the beast out of the earth. Then the angel gives the "little" book to John for him to eat and then prophesy the coming events in chapters 11-13. God is most victorious. His ways are marvelous and His thoughts are incomprehensible.

How do these ten horns relate to the harlot? In Revelation 17:16-17, these ten horns, who give full allegiance to the beast, hate the harlot. They make her desolate and naked, eat her flesh, and burn her with fire. In other words, they despise this harlot and want to destroy her; yet they participate with her in her fornication, they expose her compromise and nakedness. This very thing is also described in Ezekiel 23; (Oholah is Samaria and Oholibah is Jerusalem). Verses 5-10 describe Samaria, the capital of Israel:

> *"Ohalah played the harlot even though she was Mine;*
> *and she lusted for her lovers, the neighboring Assyrians .*
> *. . thus she committed her harlotry with them . . . and*
> *with all for whom she lusted, with all their idols, she*
> *defiled herself. I have delivered her into the hand of her*
> *lovers . . . for whom she lusted. They uncovered her*
> *nakedness, took away her sons and daughters, and slew*
> *her with the sword; she became a byword among*
> *women, for they had executed judgment on her."*

Verses 11-34 describe Jerusalem (capital of Judah):

> *"Oholibah became more corrupt in her lust and harlotry*
> *then her sister Ohalah. She looked at images of*
> *Chaldeans . . . as soon as she saw them, she lusted for*
> *them and sent messengers to them in Chaldea. Then the*

*Babylonians came to her, into the bed of love, and they
defiled her with their immorality . . . she revealed her
harlotry and uncovered her nakedness. Thus says the
Lord God to Oholibah, 'Behold, I will stir up your lovers
against you . . . and I will bring them against you from
every side. I will delegate judgment to them, and they
shall judge you according to their judgments . . . they
shall also strip you of your clothes and take away your
beautiful jewelry. Thus I will make you cease your
lewdness and your harlotry . . . I will deliver you into the
hand of those you hate . . . They will deal hatefully with
you, take away all you have worked for, and leave you
naked and bare. The nakedness of your harlotry shall be
uncovered. I will do these things to you because you
have gone as a harlot after the Gentiles, because you
have become defiled by their idols.'"*

This describes the very picture we see in Revelation 17:16-
17. God put it into the hearts of these ten 'rogue' kings to fulfill His
purpose . . . until the words of God are fulfilled. God also put it in
the heart of Assyria (Isaiah 10:5-7), and in the heart of Babylon
(Jeremiah 40:2-3) to fulfill His purpose . . . until His words were
fulfilled. Is not God free to do with His creation as He desires? God
raised up the Pharaoh for His purposes as declared in Romans 9:17
and 22.

*For the scripture says to the Pharaoh, "For this purpose
I have raised you up, that I may show My power in you.
What if God, wanting to show His wrath and to make
His power known, endured with much longsuffering the
vessels of wrath prepared for destruction, and that He
might make known the riches of His glory on the vessels
of mercy, which He had prepared beforehand for glory."*

He used the Pharaoh of Egypt and the kings of Assyria and
Babylon, and He also will use these ten kings that are associated
with the beast to discipline and scourge harlotry from His people for
the purpose of making known His riches to His own people because
of His great mercy. God also used Joseph's brothers for His own

purposes when they sold him into slavery. It was His opportunity to make known His mercy and to save them from destruction. His brothers meant it for evil, but God turned it around and used it for good. Later on, Joseph said to his brothers, *"As for you, you meant it evil against me; but God meant it for good, in order to bring it about as it is this day, to save many people alive"* (Genesis 50:20). All those who came out of Egypt died in the wilderness because of the hardness of their hearts, even though God showed them His great mercy over and over in the wilderness. He does these same things to His people today. It is of utmost importance that we find ourselves aligned with the same faith as Joshua and Caleb had after they had spied out Canaan (Numbers 13:30-33). The other ten spies gave into fear and unbelief. He loves it when we turn our gaze towards Him and endeavor to please Him even though we sometimes slip, trip, stumble and fall. God is full of mercy, yet I know that those who willfully persist in harlotry will be cut off forever. Those who repent will be purged and cleansed. The Mother of harlots (the woman sitting on the beast), is running after this beast and his kingdom thinking he is her bridegroom. Could she be deceived into thinking that this beast is the return of Jesus? Does this sound bizarre? She claims to be the bride, but is full of filth and abominations from her harlotry and will be destroyed in one hour, as we will see in Revelation 18.

# Chapter 4
# "COME OUT OF HER MY PEOPLE, LEST YOU SHARE IN HER SINS . . ."
### Revelation 18:4

## What Are We To Come Out Of?

The content of the next chapters will severely mess with your life's paradigm. You will never be the same again. What I am about to share with you in the pages of these chapters will rock the very foundation of your belief system as it did mine! If you have been in the faith for any amount of time you know that God does not change. He is always wooing us to Himself and desirous for His character to be built in us. Sometimes when the Holy Spirit reveals a mystery of God to us, it does rock the very foundation that we have built upon.

Chapter 18 starts with the picture of an angel coming down from heaven, who is no ordinary angel! This angel lights up the whole earth with the glory that is on him. By his very presence, he demands the respect of the entire world, because of the great authority God has bestowed upon him. The words that proceed from his mouth are uttered in a loud voice crying out, *"Babylon the great is fallen, is fallen, and **has become** a dwelling place of demons, a prison for every foul spirit, and a cage for every unclean and hated bird!"* The Amplified translation says (emphasis mine), *"**Has become** a resort and dwelling place for demons, a dungeon haunted by every loathsome spirit, an abode for every filthy and detestable bird!"*

The very proclamation of the words "**has become**" indicates it wasn't that way before, but digressed to this. A similar proclamation was spoken over Jerusalem by Isaiah as he addresses the unfaithfulness of the city of God's people. *"How the faithful city has become a harlot. It was full of justice; righteousness lodged in it, but now murderers."* Demons and foul spirits live in and through the power of darkness in a person's life. These people mentioned above, either do not know God or have known Him at one time and have fallen away or are following Him from a distance. John saw a woman arrayed and adorned as a bride, but now he is seeing something very different.

The words "filthy" and "detestable" bring to mind that these birds eat dead and rotting things. There is a list of unclean birds in Deuteronomy 14:12-18. Most of these birds eat things that have died and are rotting and are considered unclean or filthy. In Deuteronomy 28, there is a list of blessings and curses. Blessings in diligently obeying the voice of the Lord and being careful to observe His commands and curses if you do not do these things. One of the curses: *"Your carcasses shall be food for all the birds of the air."* Meaning you won't live long and you will die in shame with filthy birds all over your dead body consuming your flesh. Yes, this sounds somewhat morbid, but it was a truthful reality. God does not mince words, but is very intentional when He says that you will be blessed if you keep His word. Anything that is not blessed of God is dead and rotting. People of Babylon were equated with becoming filthy and detestable birds that feed on dead and rotting things. No child of God should feed their soul on the dead things of this world.

- Jeremiah 5:26-28: *"'Among My people are found wicked men; they lie in wait as one who sets snares; they set a trap; they catch men. As a cage is full of birds, so their houses are full of deceit. Therefore they have become great and grown fat, they are sleek; yes they surpass the deeds of the wicked."*
- Jeremiah 7:33: *"The corpses of this people will be food for the birds of the heaven . . . and no one will frighten them away."*
- Revelation 19:21: *And all the birds fed ravenously and glutted themselves with their flesh.*
- Matthew 24:28: *"Wherever there is a fallen body* (a corpse), *there the vultures (or eagles) will flock together".* The fallen body, mentioned by Jesus, refers to verse 23, *"If anyone says to you, 'Look, there is the Christ, do not believe it. For false Christ's will rise and show great signs and wonders to deceive . . . even the **elect**."*

Filthy and detestable birds feed on dead things; which are false Christ's as Jesus just indicated! This is again another picture of the woman (Babylon, the Mother of Harlots) who is adorned and arrayed as a bride. She has been fully won over and deceived by this beast. We must remember that the great Babylon, or woman, is a representation of many people from all walks of life; from every nation and language. The beast mentioned is a representation of a false messiah/Christ. In fact, this beast could pose as the return of Jesus Christ. Revelation 17:8 says, *". . . they will marvel when they see the beast that was, and is not, and yet is."* Our Lord is described in the previous chapter as *". . . the One who is and who was and who is to be"* (Revelation 16:5). There is a marked difference in the description of both the beast and the Lord. The woman is being carried by this beast and has given herself fully to him deceiving all people. This is described in Revelation 18:3, *"For all nations have drunk of the wine of the wrath of her fornication, the kings of the earth have committed fornication with her, and the merchants of the earth have become rich through the abundance of her luxury."* She has an affect on all nations by enticing and willingly presenting her harlotry to kings, leaders, dictators, presidents, monarchs, prime ministers, etc. She is the great city which reigns over the kings of the earth (Revelation 17:18) and has also become like a cage full of filthy and detestable birds. This drama is being played out before our very eyes!

The last Scripture in Chapter 17 says, *"and the woman whom you saw is that great city which reigns over the kings of the earth."* The woman that John had seen described in Revelation 17:1-5 is the same woman that reigns over the kings of the earth. The harlot bride arrayed and adorned is the "great city." Looking back to the days of ancient Babylon, she ruled an area about half the size of Texas. In order to observe in this present day situation what it looks like to reign over the kings of the earth, we must go out on a much broader scale. At present, I only know of one nation that pretty much dominates the rest of the world. Through technology and tremendous advanced fire power, "this" nation rules over all the other nations. You might argue this point, but in reality it is very true. We must have a world vision, a revelation that goes beyond our own lives her in the US.

48

## Come Out of Iniquity! Stop the Lawlessness!

*"Her sins have reached to heaven, and God has remembered her iniquities,"* (Revelation 18:5). This word iniquity is found throughout Scripture. One such place is Psalm 32:5, where King David confesses to God, *"I acknowledged my sin to You, and my iniquity I have not hidden. I said, 'I will confess my transgressions to the Lord, and You forgave the iniquity of my sin.'"* Here in this verse, we find that the word iniquity has different meaning then the word sin. Romans 3:23 says, *For all have sinned and fall short of the glory of God.* All have sinned, but who are the ones who commit iniquity? What is iniquity? Again Psalm 103:10 separates sin from iniquity, *He has not dealt with us according to our sins, nor punished us according to our iniquities.* Iniquity is described very plainly in Ezekiel 18:24-26, *"When a righteous man turns from his righteousness and commits iniquity, and does according to all the abominations that the wicked man does . . . When a righteous man turns away from his righteousness, commits iniquity and dies in it, it is because of the iniquity which he has done that he dies."* When someone turns from righteousness and walks in the way of the wicked, he commits iniquity. Iniquity is the willful decision of the righteous to commit sin.

So when Babylon, the harlot fornicator has fallen, she has willfully turned away from righteousness, has followed the way of the wicked, and has become . . . a cage full of hated birds. Jeremiah 31:34 (emphasis mine) says, *"I will forgive their **iniquity**, and their sin I will remember no more."* Just a note: Even when we commit iniquity, if our gaze turns back upon Him and remains, then we will experience forgiveness. The writer of Hebrews quotes Jeremiah 31:34 in Hebrews 8:12 and 10:17 (emphasis mine), *"And their sins and their **lawless deeds** I will remember no more."* The writer of Hebrews uses the words **lawless deeds** in place of the word **iniquity**; so lawless deeds and iniquity are one and the same. Jesus points this out when He confronts the scribes and Pharisees in Matthew 23:28, *"Even so you also outwardly appear righteous to men, but inside you are full of hypocrisy and lawlessness."* The scribes and Pharisees were the representation of God in those days. They were not heathen or Gentile sinners; they were to be representing righteous living. Jesus points out that they are full of lawlessness.

Again, what is lawlessness? It is the willful decision to reject God's Word or voice and do what we want because of selfish ambition or fear of man. The harlot is lawless! She says in her heart, *"I sit as queen, and am no widow, and will not see sorrow"*. She looks good on the outside, but her sins and lawlessness are piled high up to heaven. She is a habitual committer of iniquity. Paul addresses the iniquity of certain people who claim they are brothers in the Lord. *"I have written to you not to keep company with anyone named a brother, who is sexually immoral, or covetous, or an idolater, or a reviler, or a drunkard, or an extortioner--not even to eat with such a person"* (1 Corinthians 5:11). They were lawless and Paul even goes one step further in addressing a list of people (1 Corinthians 6:9-11) who habitually and willfully commit iniquity and says these will not inherit the Kingdom of God. He's addressing believers that were cheating their own brethren. He then re-asks: *"Do you not know that the unrighteous will not inherit the kingdom of God? Do not be deceived. Neither fornicators, nor idolaters, nor adulterers, nor homosexuals, nor sodomites, nor thieves, nor covetous, nor drunkards, nor revilers, nor extortioners will inherit the kingdom of God. And such were some of you. But you were washed, but you were sanctified, but you were justified in the name of the Lord Jesus and by the Spirit of our God."* If you remain in these sins, even if you claim you are a believer, you will not inherit the kingdom of God.

We must ask ourselves if we are lawless in our actions and responses to God. How often do we hear the voice of God and reject it because we are too busy or don't like something that He says? We turn a deaf ear to God because it is not convenient and to pursue what we want. We are in pursuit of things like the "American Dream", luxury, pleasure, and prosperity. All of these pursuits equate to idolatry. How often do we choose the pleasures of this world over doing what God said? When God says to us, "Don't go to that movie, because you will see wickedness", do we ignore His voice and see it anyway? God speaks and we ignore. How many times can we ignore God's voice and still have a sensitive heart towards God? Another example would be when we lie to others. It's just a little lie (in our estimation), but we just said it to make ourselves look good. Afterwards (if we have a sensitive heart), God will tell us immediately that we just told a lie. If we humble ourselves and make it right we walk in integrity. If we ignore the conviction because of our lie, we ignore God's voice and commit iniquity. Revelation 21:7-8 addresses this: *"He who overcomes shall inherit all things . . . but the cowardly, unbelieving, abominable, murderers, sexually immoral, sorcerers, idolaters, and all liars shall have their part in the lake of fire. . . "* It's interesting that cowards, the unbelieving, and liars are in this list of horrific sins.

There is a difference if we realize what we have done, repent, and seek His forgiveness. Repentance is an ongoing mindset and not an isolated decision that changes the next day! If we continue in our resistance of God's voice and continuously pursue our own desires and pleasures, we will eventually end up creating a god of our own making. Satan loves to see this happen! The ultimate results of this pursuit of lawlessness will bring about the 'lawless one' who will marvel mankind with himself and his deceptive powers. The beast is man's own creation of a god because of man's own lawless pursuits.

Satan sees this lawlessness and accommodates man by creating a god or image for him to worship. Thus we see a beast full of blasphemy, claiming to be God! Jesus highlights a characteristic of Satan when Peter rebukes Jesus because He says He's going to be killed. He turned to Peter and said, *"Get behind Me, Satan! You are an offense to Me, for you are not mindful of the things of God, but the things of men."* Jesus was not talking to Peter; He was talking to Satan. He revealed that Satan is mindful of the things of men, so he works his magic and creates a god. The entire world is looking for a savior; a political figure who will create and establish laws and reform to eventually bring about world harmony and happiness. One who will stand in as a god to bring world peace with all the benefits. Only this god will completely enslave the entire world and bring much sorrow on mankind. We must remember, the angel had a little book; a short story; three and one half years! Thank God He told us in advance!

## Stop Being a Stumbling Block!

I would like to re-emphasize the harlot has made the inhabitants of the earth drunk with the wine of her fornication (Revelation 17:2). In chapter 19:2, it says *". . . He has judged the great harlot who corrupted the earth with her fornication . . ."* She has presented a lifestyle modeled before the entire earth. One that has not led them to truth, but has actually corrupted and made people lust for her lifestyle. She is a counterfeit! She has led the way to destruction! There came a voice from heaven saying, *". . . Come out of her My people . . . Render to her just as she rendered to you, and repay her double according to her works, . . . "* (Revelation 18:4, 6). As she has corrupted the way with her fornication, so will be her destruction; and even more: *" . . . repay her 'double' according to her works . . . "*

We must learn to love what God loves and hate what God hates! God hates this corruption and harlotry. He hates compromise. He hates, with perfect and clean hatred, those who would cause others to stumble. We see this righteous hatred towards lawlessness written throughout the pages of Scripture from Genesis all the way through the prophets and the New Testament! Jesus addresses it again in Matthew 7:22-23 saying, *"Many will say to Me in that day, 'Lord, Lord, have we not prophesied in Your name, cast out demons in Your name, and done many wonders in Your name? And then I will declare to them, 'I never knew you; depart from Me, you who practice lawlessness!'"*

How can someone who prophesies and who does miracles in His name be lawless? Like the Pharisees, do these people only look righteous on the outside, yet their hearts are full of lawlessness? Jesus also speaks a hard word in Matthew 18:6, *"Whoever causes one of these little ones who believe in Me to sin, it would be better for him if a millstone were hung around his neck, and he were drowned in the depth of the sea."*

Many would say right here, "That's my uncle (or fill in the blank with who it might be for you). He is always trying to get us to do evil things." This might be true, but there is an evil far worse than your uncle. If your lifestyle and desires are worldly, even though you strongly claim to walk with God, you may cause a new believer with a weak conscience to sin. You have just become a stumbling block with a millstone attached to you. You cannot speak one thing and have your lifestyle and desires show another. Nothing is more offensive to God and man than someone proclaiming Jesus and being persistently filled with the filth of the world. This is hypocrisy. If in this we find conviction in our hearts, it shows we still have a conscience and there is still hope for us. *"... Come out of her ... "* and press hard after God.

# Chapter 5
# "COME OUT OF HER MY PEOPLE . . . LEST YOU RECEIVE OF HER PLAGUES."
### Revelation 18:4

" . . . *She says in her heart, 'I sit as queen, and am no widow, and will not see sorrow.' Therefore her plagues will come in one day--death, and mourning and famine. And she will be utterly burned with fire, for strong is the Lord God who judges her,"* (Revelation 18:7-8). God is going to use these ten kings to bring judgment upon the harlot. Back in Revelation 17:16 it says," *The ten horns which you saw on the beast, these will hate the harlot, make her desolate and naked, eat her flesh and burn her with fire."* The next verse is key to this: *"For God has put it into their hearts to fulfill His purpose, to be of one mind, and to give their kingdom to the beast, until the words of God are fulfilled."* He uses these kings and brings His fire upon her (to be utterly burned with fire) in one day! I believe this could happen through a potential nuclear explosion. I used to look at these things in Revelation and see them as if I would be watching a Hollywood movie. They just didn't strike me as reality. Seeing in the news today that Iran is seeking to enrich uranium for the purpose of a nuclear warhead makes all this very real. Iran continuously threatens America and Israel with complete destruction and proclaims, "All praise to Allah," at the same time. It has been said that Iran will have nuclear capabilities in one year. Being that this was said three years ago, I'm finding it hard to believe that Iran doesn't already have a nuclear weapon.

## Tyre---The City of Merchandise!

Before we continue in Revelation on the judgment of the Great Babylon Harlot, there are Scriptures in the prophets that must be considered. Let's look in the book of Ezekiel as God addresses Tyre and how this city was lifted up and exalted, but then brought down very swiftly. If God's people are to come out of the harlot, spoken of in the book of Revelation, then they should be aware of the things that this harlot has given herself to. It seems to be clear in Scripture what her sins are; so the following Scriptures concerning Tyre will help to understand God's heart towards the harlot. I will leave the conclusions up to the reader.

Tyre's attitude towards Israel, was one that took advantage of her fall to become increasingly wealthy and powerful. Ezekiel reveals some incredible statements about this city.

> "Son of man, because Tyre has said against Jerusalem, 'Aha! She is broken who was the gateway of the peoples; now she is turned over to me; I shall be filled; she is laid waste.' Therefore thus says the Lord God; 'Behold, I am against you, O Tyre and will cause many nations to come up against you," (Ezek. 26:2-3).

> "Because you have set your heart as the heart of a god, behold, therefore, I will bring strangers against you, the most terrible of the nations . . . **You were the seal of perfection**, full of wisdom and perfect in beauty. **You were in Eden**, the garden of God; Every precious stone was your covering . . . You were the anointed cherub who covers; I established you; you were on the holy mountain of God; you walked back and forth in the midst of fiery stones. **You were perfect** in your ways from the day you were created, **till iniquity was found** in you. By the abundance of your **trading** you became filled with violence within, and you sinned . . . Your heart was lifted up because of your beauty. You defiled your sanctuaries by the multitude of you iniquities, **by the iniquity of your trading,"** (Ezek.28:7, 12-18 emphasis mine).

Ezekiel highlights that Tyre had a similar attitude as Babylon did in the book of Revelation. Tyre lusted for Israel's down fall, because then she could be exalted and become the prominent city. Babylon is drunk with the blood of the saints and martyrs of Jesus pursuing their downfall, because they are exposing her iniquity and sin. This portion of Scripture also seems to be addressing more than just Tyre. It seems to be addressing Satan's character and his attitude which manifested in Tyre. Notice verse 13 (emphasis mine), *"You were in **Eden** the garden of God."* Tyre was not in Eden. Verse 14 (emphasis mine) says, *"You were the anointed cherub who covers . . . You walked back and forth in the midst of fiery stones.* ***You were perfect in your ways from the day you were created."*** Perfect until iniquity was found. Was the king of Tyre ever perfect? Was the king of Tyre an anointed cherub who covers? Tyre/Satan sinned because of the abundance of trading. Trading what, you might ask? It seems that Tyre/Satan were immersed in merchandising (trading rooted in a lust for power to succeed) which caused them to sin. Becoming filled with violence, God cast him out of the mountain of God. His heart was lifted up because of his beauty and was corrupted because of his splendor as the Scripture indicates. It also says that he defiled his sanctuaries because of the multitude of his iniquities; the iniquity of trading. This portion of Scripture seems to address more than just Tyre. Again, we find in the book of Nahum 3:16 a reference to merchandising and trading: *"You have multiplied your merchants more than the stars of heaven. The locust plunders and flies away."* Nahum speaks of Nineveh which was the capital of Assyria. Assyria was a world power and had brought destruction upon Israel. Assyria was then conquered by Babylon about 100 years later. Here she is described as being full of merchants and the merchants are equated to plundering locusts. What a descriptive word picture this is. You will see in Nahum 3:4, that Nineveh was compared to a harlot that was steeped in using sorcery. *"Because of the multitude of harlotries of the seductive harlot, the mistress of sorceries, who sells nations through her harlotries, and families through her sorceries."* These two things (merchandizing and harlotry/sorcery) are spoken of as working together hand in hand. These same two things are also spoken of in Revelation chapters 17 and 18. You might find this simplistic, but it is all there in Scripture to study out. I must ask you; did God set up this worlds system the way it is today? You will see in the next few verses that the merchandise that was traded in Tyre could be compared to what is traded today.

*"Now, son of man, take up a lamentation for Tyre, and say to Tyre, 'You who are situated at the entrance of the sea, merchant of the peoples ... Tarshish was your merchant because of your many* **luxury goods** *... Javan, Tubal, and Meshech were your traders. They bartered human lives ... Togarmah traded horses ... Syria traded emeralds, purple ... corals and rubies ... Judah traded wheat, honey, oil and balm. Damascus was your merchant because of the abundance of goods you made, because of your many* **luxury items** *... Kedar ... traded with you in lambs, rams, and goats. The merchants of Sheba and Raamah were your merchants. They traded for your wares the* **choicest spices**, *all kinds of* **precious stones**, *and* **gold** *... The ships of Tarshish were carriers of your merchandise.* (Ezek. 27:2-25)

Some would say, "So what! Everybody trades. We can't live without trade." Trade is what this world is set up for at the present time. This wasn't the divine design from the beginning. Just the fact that there was perfection **till** iniquity was found, and through the abundance of trade, violence manifested which resulted in sin (Ezekiel 28:16). There came a lust for luxury and comfort of which Satan accommodated. He made it very obtainable for everyone, even God's chosen people! The great corruptor of man: Luxury, comfort, ease along with the desire for greatness, dominance, and power.

If you compare Ezekiel chapters 26-28 with Revelation chapters 17-18 you will find many similarities between Tyre and Great Babylon. In Ezekiel 27:29-30, we read, *"All the pilots of the sea will come down from their ships and stand on the shore ... they will cry bitterly and cast dust on their heads ... they will weep for you* (Tyre) *with bitterness of heart and bitter wailing."* Why? The answer is in verses 35-36, *"Your merchandise and the entire company will fall."* There was great wealth exchanged and when it came to an end there was very strong emotion; bitter weeping and wailing by those who had traded with Tyre.

## Babylon---The City of Merchandise!

Now we will look to Babylon in the book of Revelation. First it says in 18:9, *"The kings of the earth . . . will weep and lament for her, when they see the smoke of her burning. Then the merchants of the earth will weep and mourn over her, for no one buys their merchandise anymore."* Is there tremendous exaggeration in the Scriptures when it says the kings and merchants weep and mourn over her? Why would God exaggerate about these things if they were not true? Think about the magnitude of this disaster! When Hurricane Sandy hit Long Island and the Jersey shore, were those who made their living from tourism all of a sudden inundated with tourists? They were devastated and not just because of the destruction of the hurricane; for even if their business was not destroyed, no one came to buy their merchandise. Revelation is talking about something of much greater magnitude than Hurricane Sandy. *"The merchants of the earth, the kings of the earth, every shipmaster, and as many as trade on the sea . . . threw dust on their heads and cried out, weeping and wailing"* (verses 17-19). It sounds as if the whole world is affected by Babylon's fall. No one buys their merchandise anymore. This disaster brings the trade of all luxury merchandise to an end. Their income has been cut off forever! The demand or ability to obtain these things has come to an end forever. The law of supply and demand has just been obliterated in Babylon's destruction forever. Could this be the prelude to no buying and selling without the mark of the beast? Could this be the sixth trumpet judgment in which one-third of man-kind are all killed (described in more detail)?

There is a list of merchandise in verses 12-13 of chapter 18 which seems so limited to us who have such a far greater selection to choose from in this age. This merchandise was of great value back then and the demand for it was great; yet today the demand seems to be out of control with no end in sight. We have become inundated with merchandise.

*"Merchandise of gold and silver, precious stones and pearls . . . "*

Have you been in Jared's or Helzberg's or even big box stores such as Wal-Mart? In this day and age it would be hard to find someone who had not gone into one of these stores. We have billions of dollars of merchandise just in jewelry alone. Thousands of stores carry this merchandise; however, it's not just displayed in jewelry cases at these stores, but on the body parts of the people who buy it as well.

> *"Merchandise of . . . fine linen and purple, silk and scarlet . . . "*

Macy's, Herberger's, and hundreds of stores sell billions and billions of dollars of fine clothing, bedding, towels, rugs, drapery, etc. Oh, and did I mention clothing? Yes, I did. From prom gowns to lingerie (which, by the way, is always strategically positioned in the middle of the store so that it can't be avoided). This intimate apparel display has to be a major stumbling block to every man and boy that walks by. The middle of the store has its idol on display for all to see. What are we teaching our teenagers about sexuality, as their hormones are raging within them?

> *"Merchandise of every kind of citron wood, every kind of object of ivory, every kind of object of most precious wood, bronze, iron, and marble . . . "*

Have you walked into a home improvement store lately? Doors made of any kind of wood to be desired. Beautiful magnificent windows, countertops of granite, flooring made of luxury stone, and cabinets made of oak, cherry, bamboo or any other exotic wood. Carpeting can be purchased from one dollar per square foot all the way up to one hundred dollars or more per square foot. There's even a store that only carries furniture and accessories from the 50's. This is just a fraction of the merchandise carried by these stores. Homeowners love it and we fill our homes with any and everything that you could ever imagine. Having worked in hundreds of homes, I've seen merchandise from the inexpensive to the very expensive; from the simple to the very exotic--coming from all parts of the world. There seems to be everything available for our homes these days, even things beyond our wildest imagination.

*"Merchandise of cinnamon and incense, fragrant oil and frankincense . . . "*

I was made very aware of this merchandise when my wife and I went to a mall a few months ago and walked through Herberger's perfume and makeup department. It was massive. I could smell almost every perfume that was being displayed. I thought I was smelling my aunt, grandmother, and everyone else's aunt and grandmother all at the same time. It was overwhelming. America spends $4.2 billion on perfume per year[3]. The perfume and makeup industry are aimed at defining what beauty should be for women (and men). Through marketing, TV, and movies, beauty is dictated to us and teaches dissatisfaction, seduction, and jealousy towards others. I've heard it preached that one of the greatest enemies we have is in our own home: the mirror. It tells us we are not good enough or beautiful enough or strong enough. It tells us we are ugly, overweight, too tall, too short, etc, etc, etc. It lies to us every time we look at it. This enemy must fall.

*"Merchandise of wine . . . "*

Seen any liquor stores lately? Any kind of mind bending liquid (or liquor) that your heart (or flesh) desires can be purchased. Anyone heard of the term "Margarita Ville", (of which many believers also participate)? Maybe you have heard of the biography, *God and Guinness: A Biography of a Beer That Changed the World*. How does beer change the world for righteousness and holiness? The latest is a group called "Beer, Bible, and Brotherhood". Drink your beer and study your Bible. Are we indulging in the flesh, all the while endeavoring to placate God by studying His Holy Word? This is not a new idea. The priest and prophet also indulged in wine and intoxicating drink. Isaiah points this out in Isaiah 28:7, *"They also have erred through wine, and through intoxicating drink are out of the way. They err in vision, they stumble in judgment."* The adult beverage has caused them to speak deception. They can't hear from God because they are under the influence. Proverbs 31:4 says, *"It is*

---

[3] http://mentalfloss.com/article/31222/numbers-how-americans-spend-their-money

*not for kings to drink wine, or for rulers to desire strong drink, lest they drink and forget the law and what it decrees, and pervert the justice due any of the afflicted"* (Amplified). This Scripture also seems to indicate that kings would err in judgment and forget the law of God if they were given to wine. I'm sure that many could find Scripture to justify their drinking, but these I have mentioned seem to bring a serious note to this subject. The story of Nadab and Abihu, Aaron's sons, is another example of erring through drink. Leviticus 10:1-2 says that they offered strange fire before the Lord, and fire went out from the Lord and devoured them. God's response was that He must be regarded as holy. In verse 10, the Lord spoke to Aaron after this happened. The Lord said, *"Do not drink wine or intoxicating drink, you, or your sons* (the two left) *when you go into the tabernacle or else you will die. This will be a statute forever . . . that you may distinguish between holy and unholy, and between unclean and clean."* Nadab and Abihu were under the influence and did something stupid which they shouldn't have and ended up being devoured by fire. Also a Nazarite, that had consecrated himself to God, was to refrain from drink and the very elements that made drink (grapes). They were set apart for holiness all the days of their consecration. Paul comes out and declares in his letter to the Ephesians (5:18), *"Do not be drunk with wine, for that is debauchery"* (Amp). Debauchery is the seduction from virtue. Paul finishes his statement with, *" . . . but be filled with the Spirit."* If drink causes debauchery or seduction from virtue, then I would think that every named child of God would run from this as far as he could; never to drink again!

*"Merchandise of oil, fine flour, wheat, cattle, sheep . . . "*

Grocery store chains are big business these days. Even the gas stations are selling groceries. Everything from ring pops to canned octopus. We sell it all! What would happen if the electrical grid was damaged severally and the power was off for two to three weeks or more? What would life look like without electricity? We don't even give this a second thought. Electricity is like second nature to us. We so take it for granted till we don't have it, then we run around frantically realizing all the benefits of this luxury. I must ask a question at this point; "Will we always have electricity on this planet?" After six to seven thousand years of not having it, and then all of a sudden, in the past one hundred years it has exploded over most of the world, doesn't that seem somewhat unusual? Doesn't it seem like something major is about to happen to change the course of history? Just saying . . .

*"Merchandise of horses and chariots . . . "*

Today there are vehicles for work, travel, war, and pleasure. Seen any new car dealerships lately? Uncountable makes and models of pleasure vehicles available. Vehicles for work or war (armored military humvee's and tanks) are also available. Chariots with horsepower but without the horses. Everyone has a chariot these days! Most families have 2 or 3 chariots and a three car garage to put them in, plus room for all the toy chariots. Chariots from the super customized to the dented and rusty! Billions and billions of dollars of merchandise. Raising livestock of cattle, sheep, and horses is also big business. Horses were used (can be used today) for work purposes, but most likely used for recreation or profit. I would also like to point out something that is closer to home for most people. Pets are a big industry today. A person can spend hundreds, even up to thousands just to own one pet. Americans spend $61.4 billion a year on their pets[4]. I love the pets we have, but to say that a smelly, slobbering, poop eater is man's best friend doesn't say a whole lot about the man. His priorities are way off.

*"Merchandise of bodies and souls of men . . ."*

Millions of people are trafficked for profit as slaves for labor, servitude, and the sex trade industry. Bodies of little 5 year old girls and boys are being used in the sex trade industry, some born to the mothers ensnared in it. Girls as young as 10 & 12 are also being sold into the sex trade as prostitutes. THIS IS AN ABOMINATION! Human trafficking for the sex trade industry is big business today. Every thirty seconds another victim becomes enslaved in sex trafficking. The average age is 12 years old. There are 27,000,000 people trapped in slavery throughout the world;

---

[4] Msn money partner, May 21, 2013, by Vickie Elmer

100,000 in America alone[5]. Of all the victims, 99% are not rescued. Young children, as well as young adults are being captured and used to make billions of dollars. There are documentaries that are available on this subject if you want to be more informed. One documentary is called *Nefarious, Merchant of Souls*.[6] When I first heard that this was a national problem, I was shocked and in unbelief, "This can't be a problem today. Surely, we have gone beyond slavery!" Then I started hearing about this more through the news and ministries that were engaged in rescuing those who had been enslaved. I realized the worldview that I had didn't go beyond the borders of the US. It has just been brought to my attention that sex trafficking is a major issue at the Super Bowl. The trafficking of young women (a father's daughter) who have been captured and enslaved into this industry by no choice of their own, are being exploited, right under our noses, at an event where much celebration and frivolity is taking place. Most people that went to the Super Bowl or watched it on TV were oblivious to this activity going on behind the scenes. Have we become so dull and hardened in our hearts to the needs of the enslaved that we ignore their plight? If we knew this was going on and didn't pray for God's justice, then we are guilty ourselves! My question is, "How patient is God?" Does this twisted perversion go unnoticed by Him; this lust for power and complete dominance of an individual life? Is there still someone, somewhere that is becoming fascinated with Jesus and repenting of their wickedness, and this very thing captures the heart of God so that God withholds His wrath just a little while longer in spite of this evil? Yes, He is holding back fire and end time judgment so that more people will come into His holiness. I'm reminded of 2 Peter 3:9, *"The Lord is not slack concerning His promise, as some count slackness, but is long-suffering toward us, not willing that any should perish but that all should come to repentance."*

His promise is that He *is* coming soon and the heavens and the earth are being reserved for fire until the day of judgment (2 Peter 3:4-7). He is **patient**. The book of Revelation highlights this in chapter 1:9 (emphasis mine), *"I, John both your brother and*

---

[5] http://www.thea21campaign.org/content/the-facts/gjekag?permcode=gjekag
[6] www.nefariousdocumentary.com

*companion in the . . . **patience** of Jesus Christ . . ."* He notes that
Jesus is patient. He could bring judgment at any time. If He were
like me (which thankfully He is not), He would see all these things
happening in the world and bring it all to an end. I see only a micro-
fraction of what is happening in the world. He sees it all. All at
once, including everything that is done in secret. He sees your
decision either for holiness or wickedness, in the secret place. The
public arena is where we live out our secret place decisions and He
knows it all. It is all open and bare to Him who sees all things.
Nothing is hidden! How He can take in all this wickedness in the
world and still be patient is a great wonder to me! He also sees you
in the secret place: the one who is gazing at Him with love and
fascination. When you give Him your gaze He dances wildly for
joy! He proclaims to all the angels, "They are seeking My face. I
will show them My glory!"

## Millstones and Stumbling Blocks!

We touched on Matthew 18:6 in the previous chapter
concerning stumbling blocks and causing someone who believes to
sin. The same is portrayed when John sees a mighty angel take up a
stone like a millstone and throw it into the sea. **Millstones** and
**stumbling blocks** go hand in hand. This angel in 18:21 says while
he is throwing the millstone into the sea, *"Thus with violence the
great city Babylon shall be thrown down, and shall not be found
anymore."* Babylon is portrayed as a stumbling block! She is
causing others who believe in Jesus to stumble by her very lifestyle.
The list that follows is people and things that will not be found or
heard in great Babylon anymore because they are stumbling blocks.
Their very lifestyles are contrary to the Kingdom of God, yet they
proclaim to know the way.

> *"The sound of harpists, musicians, flutists, and
> trumpeters shall not be heard in you anymore"*
> (Revelation 18:22).

The list could also have guitarists, drummers, pianists,
organists, synthesizers, effects; screamers, country, contemporary, R

and B, hip hop, all kinds of genres. These are not just secular genres. There are many Christian songs and musicians that do not have the holiness of God on their music. Their lives are full of self-importance and motivated by lust and greed as well as many other sins. Sensitivity to God will help discern the holy from the profane. Not all Christian music is holy. Not all Christian music brings you into the presence of God. What is in the heart will come out and will always make itself known. Some seemingly great Christian songs were written by a cussing musician. It doesn't matter what genre the music is. If the Spirit isn't in the song, no matter how skillfully played or even if it is a beautiful, melodic love song, it is empty and dead. It will never be replayed in eternity. I know this is strong language to some, but we who claim His name have lost our discernment as a Church. The spirit of death has come in through the secular and has pillaged His people ever so secretly. We must regain Holy Spirit discernment in order to survive the last days. Where there is no discernment there is no fear of the Lord.

For many years I had listened to Christian rock and roll. I would listen to it at a very high volume! I would be the one who pulled up next to you at the stop light, in my car with the music pounding like thunder out of the open windows. You might think this was immature, but I actually thought it motivated me to live for Jesus more extremely. I found out later, after many years of this practice, that I was mostly motivated by the music and not the message. I carried my past lifestyle into my Christ-walk. Radical means pick up your cross. Radical is not being sub-culture for Jesus. Don't get me wrong, God uses loudness. He always has and always will. Count how many times the word "loud" is in the Book of Revelation.

The point I'm trying to make is that a believer should be full of discernment and not accept anything just for face value. Not all is holy that says it's holy! My wife shared a Scripture with some old friends that we had taken to IHOP-KC. I think it says it all? *"Then those who feared the Lord spoke to one another, and the Lord listened and heard them; so a book of remembrance was written before Him for those who fear the Lord and who meditate on His name . . . Then you shall again discern between the righteous and the wicked, between one who serves God and one who does not serve Him "* (Malachi 3:16, 18). We must have discernment in these last days. It is of major importance! I should point out that music is used in almost every situation we encounter. A movie--it would be boring without music. A restaurant or bar--it would not be exciting to frequent these places without it. In fact almost every restaurant has music piped into the bathroom so you can be soothed while relieving yourself. I would have to ask if women (and some men) would cry during a movie if there were no music in the background during a sensitive scene? Home improvement stores; home goods stores; furniture stores; hotels; even some gas stations have music to sooth the soul. *"It will not be heard in her anymore."*

> *"No craftsman of any craft shall be found in you anymore"* (Revelation 18:22).

I touched on this under the merchandise section, yet I would like to point out something that bothers me extremely. It is how Christianity has merchandised itself in such a way that we now have trinkets to T-shirts with a message; hundreds of trinkets for adults as well as children. We have cheapened our message by merchandising it! Pencils with a message. Erasers with a message. Gum with a message. Even chocolate crosses to be eaten at Easter. What does this teach our children about picking up our cross and following Jesus? Is the cross just something that tastes good? I have been an artist for years and used to sell my pictures fairly regular. I've made Christian message T-shirts and craft items, etc., to sell. I'm just as guilty as anyone for merchandizing God. I see beautiful artwork and appreciate it, yet it still is empty. I would rather appreciate the creator in the midst of His creation, because in it is life. He created it. It's not a creation of man. The world is so full of craftsmen. Every kind of merchandise you could ever desire. Merchandise, merchandise, merchandise and more merchandise. Every store that you walk into these days has millions of items of merchandise made by craftsmen. Just a side note: In the beginning God said to 'freely eat' of any tree in the garden. After the fall, man merchandized everything. This happened after Cain killed Abel and went out of the presence of the Lord (Genesis 4:16). Cain was out of His presence and so was his offspring who were craftsmen, musicians and keepers of livestock (vs.20-22). Shortly after this, God said He was sorry that He had made man (Genesis 6:6). God's original design was for man to partake of His presence and provision and not to create a system of marketing that would be so abused through exorbitant pricing which will culminate as described in the third seal in Revelation 6:6, *"A quart of wheat for one days wage."* The end of the Book of Revelation declares the restoration of His provisional plan. The trees produce fruit every month, the leaves are for healing and take the water of life freely (Revelation 22:1-2, 17). Once again, does this sound simplistic? God has declared it so. Merchandizing will one day cease to exist. Again, please question the things that I say. Study them for yourself. Find out what is truth. Don't just live by a "feel good" little book of pocket promises.

> *"The sound of a millstone shall not be heard in you anymore"* (Revelation 18:22).

This could be taken different ways; but since it is in the context of musicians creating music and craftsmen developing their crafts, we can assume it is talking about food and the creation of it. Did you know that overeating is an acceptable sin in the church? Not many sermons on this subject being preached in the Church. Ezekiel 16:49 says, *"Look, this was the iniquity of your sister Sodom: She had . . . fullness of food, and the abundance of idleness."* Another warning in regard to the fullness of food: *"When you have eaten and are full--then beware, lest you forget the Lord"* (Deuteronomy 6:11-12). God was warning His people and yet, later, He also predicted that this very thing would happen to them. *"When I have brought them to the land . . . and they have eaten and filled themselves and grown fat, then they will turn to other gods . . . they will provoke Me and break My covenant"* (Deuteronomy 31:20). Fullness and forgetting God seem to go hand in hand! This country, along with other affluent nations of the world, is full of eateries and restaurants offering anything from the exotic to the fast and easy menu. We are inundated with restaurants and buffets that carry every choice tidbit we could ever imagine. Also, every grocery store has everything from cheese sticks to frozen breakfasts. Have you even taken a hard look at the soda aisle or the potato chip aisle? Brands and flavors as far as the eye can see. I'm made more aware of Luke 17: 27-28, *"They* (those in Noah and Lot's day) *ate, they drank... Until...!"* Yes, we must eat to live, but in most cases we live to eat and carry on as if the flood is not coming or the fire and brimstone will not fall. We must wake up!

> *"The light of a lamp shall not shine in you anymore..."*
> (Revelation 18:23)

Jesus spoke of John the Baptist as being a burning and shining lamp, and that the people were willing to rejoice for a time in his light (John 5:35). John let his light shine in this dark world because he had separated himself from the world and allowed God to prepare his heart as he spent time in the wilderness. He lived a fasted lifestyle and his simple, but powerful message was to repent and prepare the way of the Lord! How many believers are willing to embrace a wilderness experience with fasting and prayer so that they can live a short life introducing the Messiah and then have their head cut off? In the parable of the sower, Jesus speaks of those who would hear the word with a noble and good heart, keep it, and bear fruit. Then He says in the next verse, *"No one, when he has lit a lamp, covers it with a vessel or puts it under a bed, but sets it on a lamp stand, that those who enter may see the light."* John put his light on a lamp stand for all to see. Jesus is saying that when you hear the word and keep it, you have just lit a lamp for all to see! The word that you heard becomes a revelation to you and you begin to live it out. This is the same as with John the Baptist; he put his light out there for all to see. This is what we must do as well! The harlot will not rejoice in this light as did those who were confronted by John. The harlot will be convicted by the light because of her fornication and abominations and then she will persecute those who carry the light of Jesus.

> *"The voice of bridegroom and bride shall not be heard in you anymore"* (Revelation 18:23).

Some would think that this refers to Jesus and the church, and that their voice won't be heard in her anymore. I believe this is true, although it could just be the voice of any bride and groom. The next part of the verse seems to point out why their voice won't be heard anymore. *"For your businessmen were the great and prominent men of the earth"* (Amplified). The harlot's relationship/love affair was with the merchants and businessmen of the earth. The voices of the bride and groom will always be filled with words of love. They are exhilarated in their love for one another and lay their lives down for each other. Their spouse is more important than themselves, but that is not so with the harlot. She looks up to and respects the merchants and businessmen. She has fallen into such shallowness that she loves them for what they can do for her; how they satisfy her with the "good things" of this world. To her, they are the great men of the earth; not those who lay down their lives for loves sake. She is disillusioned and deceived. Those that live the way of love will not be found in her anymore, because there is no love in her. Matthew 24:12-13 says, *". . . and because lawlessness will abound, the love of many will grow cold. But he who endures to the end shall be saved."*

Referring again to the city of Tyre, which was a shadow of the great harlot to come, Isaiah also speaks of Tyre's love affair with her merchants. *" Tyre . . . whose merchants are princes, whose traders are the honorable of the earth?"* (Isaiah 23:8). We can also find a comparison between Tyre and a harlot in Isaiah 23:15-17, *"It will happen to Tyre as in the song of the harlot. Take a harp, go about the city, you forgotten harlot; make sweet melody, sing many songs, that you may be remembered."* She will prostitute and commit fornication with all the kingdoms of the world on the face of the earth.

Isaiah uses the phrase "in that day" so many times throughout several chapters that one might wonder if this portion of Scripture actually refers to Tyre or to another nation in the future. Chapter 24 also says, *"Behold, the Lord makes the earth empty and makes it waste . . . the land shall be entirely emptied and utterly plundered. The earth is violently broken . . . and shall totter like a hut . . . it will fall, and not rise again. It shall come to pass in that day that the Lord will punish on high the host of exalted ones. "* Again, I ask you, does the Lord exaggerate when He speaks? He makes the earth entirely emptied? Utterly plundered? It will fall and not rise again? I could see this for Chernobyl after the nuclear accident in 1986 in the Ukraine where 50,000+ people were evacuated from their homes never to return.[7] These Scriptures in Isaiah must be speaking of future events. I could write of many other portions of Scripture in Isaiah concerning these things, but God would be pleased for you to search them out.

> *"By your sorcery all the nations were deceived"*
> (Revelation 18:23).

Just as merchants today use advertisement to market their merchandise, so the harlot advertises. She puts herself out there so she can be seen and respected by men. She has bought the lie and traded the beauty of the Lord. She has trusted in her own beauty and played the harlot. What she has done is sold herself in order to attract the love and affection of others. There is much sorcery in advertisement today. Every product or service is marketed as if you can't live without it. The pharmaceutical industry advertises or markets their products as if their products will completely heal and restore your life to the point that you will live forever. Of course, they wouldn't say that outright, but they might as well. In their advertisements they give you all the detailed symptoms of your sickness or disease with the promise that you will never feel better after you take their product. This is the same with clothing, food, business products, home improvement products, cars, trucks, just about anything that is merchandised today. In the same way, the harlot advertises her lifestyle/paradigm of life. She claims that what she has is the best and the only way to live. If you fall short of it, you are not living. This is sorcery. Sorcery is the use of power gained from the assistance or control of evil spirits. You can see how well advertisements work when they influence people to buy a certain product. They think it is their own idea and it's simply not. Just as the merchandisers use sorcery to lie and exaggerate about their products, so does the harlot. It's revealed in her heart statement, *"I sit as queen, I am no widow, I will not see sorrow."* She is not who she claims she is. I would liken these things to the ideology of the American Dream. There are millions of people immigrating to the US every year. From the year 2000 to 2010 there

---

[7] http://www.iaea.org/newscenter/features/chernobyl-15/cherno-faq.shtml

was fourteen million immigrants that entered through the borders into the United States.[8] What was the drawing? There are probably many answers to this question, but only one main reason: They have pursued what has been advertised for many years now as the American Dream. I have never heard of the Russian Dream. Or the China Dream. Or the Africa Dream. Or any other dream for that matter. The pursuit of the American Dream has left many a faithful believer on the ash heap struggling to maintain the life of luxury and ease. The Lord does cause people to prosper and even to become wealthy; yet I would ask you, "Is this for your own personal satisfaction?" Our priorities are all out of whack. It's no wonder there is no power in the Church today. Everyone seems to be pursuing an ideology instead of the Lord. And then, asking the Lord to bless their ideology.

The Bible brings out a definition of sorcery through the life of Balaam. We see this story unfold in Numbers 22-25. Our main focus will be on Numbers 24:1 which says, *"Now when Balaam saw that it pleased the Lord to bless Israel, he did not go as at other times, to seek to use sorcery . . ."* Balak, who was the king of the Moabites, conspired with the elders of Midian to hire Balaam, a so-called prophet. When Balaam went with Balak to curse Israel, God was not pleased with him. The donkey (which spoke with the voice of a man) is what saved his life; yet he pursued this path anyway and God let him go. "Balaam went with Balak . . . and Balak offered oxen and sheep and sent [portions] to Balaam . . ." (Numbers 22:39-40). Balaam (who heard Gods voice) ate food sacrificed to Baal. This is why the Lord addresses the church of Pergamos (Revelation 2:14) that He has a few things against her because she allowed those in the church to hold Balaam's doctrine: participating also in the worship of demons through eating their sacrifices. Paul also addresses this very thing in 1 Corinthians 8 where he warns those who have been eating in idols temples to beware lest they become a stumbling block. Paul says, *"You cannot drink the cup of the Lord and the cup of demons; you cannot partake of the Lord's table and the table of demons"* (1 Corinthians 10:21). Balaam had Balak (a Baal worshiper) build seven altars for him, for which Balaam then

---

[8] http://en.wikipedia.org/wiki/Immigration_to_the_United_States

offered a bull and a ram on each of the altars. This very thing happened three times. The first time (Numbers 22:41) was on the high places of Baal. If he was a true prophet of God he would have walked away from this abomination. He went on in his sorcery to do this again on Mt. Pisgah (Numbers 23:14) and Mt. Peor (Numbers 23:28-29). This very activity was considered sorcery (Numbers 24:1). He knew the Lord's voice yet ate at a demon's table and endeavored to try and manipulate God by offering what he thought God would be pleased with. This is sorcery. In the same way, we try to manipulate God through our service to Him, but all the while walking in blatant sin. This is also sorcery. The Lord brings before Babylon a challenge in Isaiah 47:12:

> *"Stand now with your enchantments and sorceries . . . let the astrologers and stargazers and the monthly prognosticators stand up and save you!"*

Modern day prognostication (or prophesying of future events) could be global warming, leading to the destruction of earth. Within this, there is an endeavoring to bring awareness of a coming calamity so we can divert it before it happens, thus saving our planet from destruction. People are seeing something coming that is catastrophic, yet are not seeking God. There are also naysayers today predicting an economic crash and that we must buy gold and have a stored food supply. I'm not saying its wrong to have these, yet it is still prognostication. These "preppers" are storing up food and guns in bunkers in order to survive all of these things that are coming. The air waves are full of predictions and warnings; from asteroids hitting earth to nuclear meltdown and from giant sinkholes to earthquakes. I must say that I find it a bit humorous to hear about global warming one year and then next year only to hear that we are heading towards another ice age. In all these things our response should not be fear, but faith in our Father God! We must trust in Him only! In all these things we must have a solemn heart response towards God.

Isaiah also points out some startling similarities to Babylon in Chapter 47:5-11: *"For you shall no longer be called The Lady of Kingdoms . . . and you said, 'I shall be a lady forever' . . . therefore hear this now, you who are given to pleasures . . . who say in your heart, 'I am, and there is no one else besides me; I shall not sit as a widow, nor shall I know the loss of children;"* The Lord's response to this attitude is that she will have two things come upon her in a moment, in one day: the loss of children and widowhood because of her sorceries! In verse 12, the Lord challenged Babylon: *"Stand now with your enchantments and the multitude of your sorceries . . . let now the astrologers, the stargazers, and the monthly prognosticators stand up and save you . . ."* Our trust needs to be in the Lord. The seriousness of the situation is captured within the statement "in one hour". Judgment will come ever so swiftly and with finality! The day comes just as a thief in the night!

Below are some comparisons contrasting the difference between the harlot and the bride. You will notice in both segments that an angel of judgment made these comparisons. God will bring an increasingly defined comparison between the two as the Day of the Lord approaches.

| The Harlot<br>Revelation 17 | The Bride<br>Revelation 21 |
| --- | --- |
| The angel said, "Come I will show you the harlot." | "Come I will show you the bride." |
| He carried me away in the Spirit to the wilderness. | He carried me away in the Spirit to a great and high mountain |
| I saw a woman sitting on a scarlet beast. | I saw the great city, the holy Jerusalem descending out of heaven from God |
| The woman was arrayed in purple and scarlet | She had the glory of God |
| She was adorned with gold, precious stones and pearls | Her light was like a most precious stone, like a jasper stone, clear as crystal |
| She had in her hand a golden cup full of abominations and filth | She had a great and high wall with 12 gates and twelve angels at the gates |
| On her forehead, 'Mystery, Babylon the Great, Mother of harlots | The names of the 12 tribes of Israel written on the 12 gates |

## All of Heaven Rejoices!

There are some incredible statements made by the redeemed of the Lord in Revelation 19 referring to the harlot's judgment. The first one is found in verses 1-2, *"After these things I heard a loud voice of a great multitude in heaven, saying, 'Alleluia! Salvation and glory and honor and power belong to the Lord our God! For true and righteous are His judgments, because He has judged the great harlot who corrupted the earth with her fornication.'"* Heaven is rejoicing because she is judged. The Scripture in Proverbs 24:17 says, *"Do not rejoice when your enemy falls, and do not let your heart be glad when he stumbles; lest the Lord see it, and it displease Him, and He turn away His wrath from him."* The Lord exhorts us to not rejoice when our enemy falls, but in this case God is encouraging His people to rejoice. Look at Revelation 18:20, *"Rejoice over her, O heaven, and you holy saints and apostles and prophets, for God has avenged you on her."* Could this statement by God be a direct response to those under the altar (Revelation 6:9) who had been slain for the word of the testimony they held? The number was completed of those who would be killed as they were. They had been crying out with a loud voice, *"How long, O Lord, holy and true, until You judge and avenge our blood on those who dwell on the earth?"* God encourages rejoicing again in 19:5, *"Then a voice came from the throne, saying, 'Praise our God, all you His servants and those who fear Him, both small and great!'"*

All of heaven seems to be rejoicing after the fall and destruction of the great harlot Babylon. Remember Babylon is people. People who think they are the bride, yet they are a harlot. Revelation 19:7 (emphasis mine): *"Let us be glad and rejoice and give Him glory for the marriage of the Lamb has come and **His wife** has made herself ready."* Finally, the corruption has gone and the false is exposed. The veil is lifted and evil is brought into the light to be openly displayed; then the pure bride comes forth! *"**To her** it was granted to be arrayed . . ."* The only one that will be arrayed in wedding garments on "That Day" will be the bride. **His wife** has made herself ready! She picked up her cross and she laid down her life. She repented and turned when she sinned. She washed her robe in the blood of the Lamb.  She overcame!  And now she lives with Him forever!  Don't you just love Jesus for what He has done and prepared for you?

# Chapter 6
# IS HE STANDING AT THE DOOR?
# GET READY!

I'm a painter by trade and have my own business. I have no PHD or formal training in Eschatology. I have been a believer since 1971 and spent the first 20 years of my Christian walk living in a community with other "Jesus People". My first experiences with sharing my faith happened in the summer of 1972 after accepting Jesus as my Lord. A group of "Jesus People" from Spokane, Washington, came to Des Moines, Iowa. I went out on the downtown streets with them and experienced the most radical style of evangelism. We would walk with businessmen for blocks sharing Jesus with them because they were too busy to stop and talk to us. The streets of downtown Des Moines were never the same from that day on!

These years were spent in evangelism of every kind: from preaching outside of Jehovah's Witness' conventions to being spit on and having tracts burnt in front of our face at Kiss concerts; from visiting prisoners in prison to preaching Jesus on Bourbon Street during the Mardi Gras on Fat Tuesday. Which, by the way, is the most insane place I have ever been in my life--although this year (2014) I had flashbacks when we went to the LGBTQ festival and parade to share Jesus. Definitely shades of Mardi Gras insanity to be seen by all! We did outreach from open air skits at Pella (home of Iowa's tulip festival), to being threatened by carnies at county fairs as they tried to run us out of town. I must point out that God is faithful when we put our trust in Him as we preach the gospel. At one point of our ministry, we went into triple xxx porn shops to talk to the employees or even the owners. Keeping your eyes on the person you are talking to is of utmost importance in these situations. If you are not talking to someone at the moment all you can do is stair at the floor. We also did a lot a bar witnessing every weekend. In these situations you have to scream over the music in order to talk to someone. God was faithful to us in our outreaches; in fact, I would have never met, Sandy, my wife, if we hadn't been in the bar sharing Jesus. So from door to door and from town to town, in winter and in summer (20 degrees below zero to 110 above), we did this for 20 years and learned very much about people, their lifestyles, and belief systems. Yes, I was considered "one of those" crazy Jesus followers that would always greet you on the street corner with the words "God loves you very much" and then always leave you with the words "Jesus is coming soon!" You would be greeted with God's love and then encountered by His soon coming in order to invoke the fear of the Lord; that you might repent.

In the community which I lived, we had teaching on deliverance, being filled with the Holy Spirit, and what it means to be a disciple. We had Old Testament and New Testament survey classes, leadership training courses, classes on counseling and church growth. There was training on the gifts of the Holy Spirit and how to walk in them. Everyone was required to take a course on Watchman Nee's book entitled *Spiritual Authority*, which did give insight and understanding on what submission to authority looked like in an age of rebellion. There were seminars on inner and physical healing, worship symposiums, evangelism explosion courses and how to make goals and see them fulfilled. We were well equipped for every good work. These were all very good, yet we didn't have much teaching on Eschatology. We just knew that Jesus could come back at any given moment and you didn't want to be in the midst of doing something stupid when He did.

I've come to the realization in the past five years that from Genesis to Revelation, there is a consistent theme and direction progressively moving towards an intentional end result which has been revealed in the book of Revelation. There are no isolated incidents in Scripture. They all point to God's intended results in the end; the consummation of the ages leading to the eradication of evil and the reign of Christ Jesus forevermore!

Six years ago, while living in Minnesota, my wife and I had an awakening in our lives. We had been faithful to God, but did not have much intimacy with Him. We went to a "Onething" Regional Conference sponsored by IHOP-KC (International House of Prayer) which is based in Kansas City, Missouri. We have never been the same since. You could say that God wrecked our lives from that moment on! The 2008 presidential elections had recently finished and what I saw as a result of it caused me to wonder if we were living close to Jesus' return. Mike Bickle (leader of IHOP-KC) was going to teach on the Book of Revelation during the Onething Conference that year being held in Kansas City, so I decided to read this book again. I haven't stopped reading it since. I've also discovered that the entire Bible is confirmed by this prophetic word from Jesus.

As a result, I have spent the last six years saturating in the Word, rising between 4 and 5 a.m. to study every morning for several hours. I'm not trying to lift myself up or brag; I'm just sharing what the Lord impressed on me to do. I wanted to be faithful to what He was saying. At first I felt like a fool, studying this book over and over. Satan would speak words of discouragement to me and tell me, "No one will listen to you! You will look like a fool!" But I wanted to obey God more than save face, so I pressed on. Some days, when I didn't have work in my painting business, I would study about 4-5 hours completely awed by God and His mysteries. Then I would share what I learned with my wife, trying to hold back the tears because of God's mysteries being opened up to me. I didn't want to read or hear about other people's teachings on the book of Revelation simply because I wanted God to speak to me and reveal His mysteries without the influence of others. I knew in the future I would begin to listen to others and their understanding of the book, which would either confirm or disapprove what I had received.

After 4 years of this intense study, I began to listen to other teachings on the book of Revelation and the last days. I remained open and receptive and some confirmed what I had received. These confirmations were not sought out, but I would hear someone teaching on this subject and their word would bring confirmation. Doesn't the Spirit of God work this way? I've found that God loves to speak and reveal Himself to His people. He's not trying to hide Himself. He does hide Himself from the rebellious and the lawless, unless they allow opening to His conviction. He will then at that time reveal Himself most gloriously. I have grown to love the Word of God and realize increasingly that Jesus means what He says in Mark 4:24, *"Be careful what you are hearing. The measure [of thought and study] you give [to the truth you hear] will be the measure [of virtue and knowledge] that comes back to you--and more [besides] will be given to you who hear"* (Amp).

If someone has good soil he will hear His voice and bear fruit. God will continue to speak in the secret place as long as we keep our soil free from offense, greed, and lust. We must fix our gaze upon Him and refuse to be distracted! He loves for us to see Him as He is: ***"The Revelation of Jesus Christ, which God gave Him to show His servants . . . "*** (emphasis mine). This is God's intent for all His servants to know this Revelation of His Son.

The things I would like to share with you in the next few paragraphs have come out of these long secret meetings with the Lord in study and seeking His face. There was a mandate from the Lord within me to understand His Word and ways more clearly. So I will endeavor to articulate the things that I received concerning the beast and the harlot. However, please don't just take my word for it, but study for yourself to see if these things be true. It would seem that a majority of believers stay away from this subject for fear of being weird or labeled a fanatic. Some seem to have their mind already made up even though they have never studied it thoroughly. They have read someone's book on the subject and swallowed it hook, line, and sinker without ever giving it a second thought. We are encouraged to grow in grace and the knowledge of Jesus Christ. Since He is coming back, I would think it would be of utmost importance to know this King; otherwise, when we stand face to face before Him on that day, He might be looking at a stranger!

## One Beast/One Law!

As I stated earlier in this book, I believe there is only one man of sin as Paul describes in 2 Thessalonians 2, and not two men or beasts as described in Revelation 13. The first beast in Revelation that comes out of the sea is the creation of Satan which I believe

81

strongly is Islam's god, Allah. The blasphemy title that the beast has is because his followers hear his voice and call him god (Allahu Akbar) or God is greater. They talk about Allah as if he is Yaweh. His followers boast, *"Who can make war with the beast?"* The reason he is called a beast is because he has the violent nature of Satan himself. Why do you think his followers are so violently against anyone who blasphemes Allah's name or turn their back on Islam and to follow Jesus? They aggressively pursue with hatred those who do these things and either imprison them or behead them. They even do these things to family members. This is what is happening at this present time in most Muslim nations. If you convert to Christianity you have committed a sin deserving death if not recanted. The Muslim Imams hate Israel and the US and talk of their destruction. Their mandate is to destroy Israel and have the UK and America live by Sharia law, for which the UK has caved already. This mandate includes Sharia being implemented throughout the entire world. Does this sound like a moderate religion? They teach this in their Mosques on a regular basis. Sharia law is a violent law of force, causing submission to what they see as holy. Thus we hear of hands being cut off or be-headings, and we see women with only their eyes showing and also being beaten if there is lack of submission. I'm sure you have also heard of honor killings, where a relative is killed for becoming too westernized or worldly.

In the early 1990's, it was shared with me by someone who was in the Navy that their ship was docked by a small town in Saudi Arabia. They were taking leave from their ship to go into the city when they were told their leave was cancelled and they all had to stay on the ship. It was cancelled due to the fact that there was going to be a public beheading in the city that night. This is Sharia law. I encourage you to please, do your homework and research these things on your own.

The second beast (Revelation 13:11) is actually the man of sin (2 Thessalonians 2:3). He is the predicted false prophet or messiah to come. I believe that this could be the messiah that all Muslims are waiting for. I must interject here that many Jews in Israel are still awaiting the Messiah after rejecting the coming of

82

Jesus Christ (pray that many find Jesus). The Sunnis and Shiites call this false messiah the Twelfth Imam or Mahdi. Shiites and Sunnis battle each other in Iraq today, yet both groups of Muslims share the hatred of Israel and her destruction. This is a crucial part of taking control in the world and bringing back the Mahdi. If you Google the word 'Mahdi' you will see more of what they believe he is and will bring to the world. When Mahmoud Ahmadinejad was president of Iran, he would pray for the return of the Mahdi every time he would speak. Here is a quote from CBN by Olivia Tulley, "Iranian President Mahmoud Ahmadinejad has been cited by various news sources as not only believing in the eventual return of the Mahdi, but that the return is near and that it is the responsibility of the Iranian government to prepare the country for his return." We know from Revelation 13 that this false prophet will perform great signs and wonders to deceive and take control. At present, Iran is endeavoring to build a nuclear weapon. Does this play into what we just talked about? Does the return of Islam's messiah go hand in glove with having a nuclear weapon in order to rule and dominate the earth? Since the sixth trumpet judgment comes from the Euphrates River area and one-third of mankind is killed (which would be over two billion people today) by fire, smoke and brimstone; obtaining a nuclear weapon is of utmost importance. Their Mahdi will be ushered into the earth through a world catastrophe.

Before we go any further we must look at some ancient Scriptures that could be a key to these things regarding Great Babylon and the beast. We go back to Genesis 10 and look at Nimrod and the beginning of his kingdom. The first city mentioned is Babel . . . in the land of Shinar. Shinar was where King Nebuchadnezzar and his god lived (Daniel 1:1-2). Also the basket with the woman in it, which was called wickedness, was carried to the land of Shinar to build a house for it. When the house is ready the basket of wickedness will be set on its base (Zechariah 5:5-11). Does this not speak of the dominance of wickedness coming from this part of the world?

The Euphrates River runs through the land of Shinar which is modern day Iraq with Iran right next to it. There are two mentions of the Euphrates River in Revelation (9:14 and 16:12). Both have a significant meaning. Revelation 16:12-14 mentions the coming of the kings and the armies of the whole world from the east (which would be Iran and beyond) gathering together in a place called Armageddon. Was the purpose of the US presence in Iraq only to create an infected open sore of hatred towards Western society? Back in Genesis 11, we see the story unfold in the building of the city of Babel. It's not just the tower of Babel as we have been taught. They were building a city and constructing a tower when the Lord saw their efforts and their attitude. They were saying, *"Come let us build ourselves a city, and a tower whose top is in the heavens; let us make a name for ourselves!"* Notice the Lord's response to this attitude, *"Behold, they are one people and they have all one language; and this is only the beginning of what they will do, and now nothing they have imagined they can do, will be impossible for them"* (Amplified). From this observation, when the Lord comes down and sees what is in the world today, especially in America's cities today; what does He say? What are His thoughts? Doesn't it seem that nothing is impossible in this day and age?

We look at ancient Babel and laugh because the city was so small and the tower did not come close in comparison to the sky scrapers we have today. But, it's so much more than just tall buildings. It's the age of technology, because of one simple little thing: electricity. It's also the age of the modern chariot, because of one thing: crude oil. And all this has come about within a 100 year period.[9] Ok, this being said, what would the Lord say about our cities today? Have we surpassed what God saw was going to happen to the people in Babel? He said, *"Nothing would be impossible for them!"* I believe it was not time for this to happen in the days of Babel. That's why the Lord came down and confused and scattered them.

The vision that Zechariah had of the basket of wickedness having a house built for it in Shinar is a prophetic sign for this region of Iraq and Iran and the drama of the last days being played out there. Zechariah also had another word: *"Behold, your King is*

---

[9] www.livinghistoryfarm.org/farminginthe30s/life_08.html and en.wikipedia.org/wiki/Ford_Model_T

*coming to you; He is just and having salvation, lowly and riding on a donkey . . . I will cut off the chariot from Ephraim and the horse from Jerusalem; the battle bow shall be cut off. He shall speak peace to the nations; His dominion shall be from sea to sea, and from the River (Euphrates) to the ends of the earth."* This scripture is not talking about the Mahdi. It is talking about the King of kings who has risen from the dead and has ascended into heaven itself to sit down at the right hand of the One who sits on the throne. Now He waits till His enemies are made a footstool for His feet. If God scattered the people of Babel, what will happen to the great Babylon harlot and the kingdom of the beast?

The description given in Revelation 17 and 18 concerning Great Babylon, the harlot, describes her as a ruler and dominating the earth. She has the attitude that she is superior in comparison to all other nations, as we see in this statement: *"I sit as queen, I am no widow, I shall not see sorrow."* Her state of morality (in her own opinion) far surpasses others. Yet, she has a dirty little secret: she hates all those who follow Jesus, but embraces all other religions. She has and presently is endeavoring to not offend any of the religions of the earth, but desires to appease all except Christianity. Crosses are being removed because they offend. Anything that has to do with Jesus will offend other religions and this cannot be tolerated. Those who love people, but point out the sins of those who are in direct disagreement with the holiness of the God of the Bible are labeled as "haters" and must be silenced. Does any of this sound familiar? Laws are being written at present to silence these people.

She (Great Babylon) is very wealthy and lives very luxuriously. Even the poor live in luxury compared to other nations (TV's, cell phones--everybody has one). Over $3 billion each year is spent on ring tones alone.[10] Merchandise is continuously being consumed by all people. You probably guessed by now that I'm referring to the United States of America. Before you react, please consider these things. We have declared ourselves a Christian nation to the rest of the world. That's how all these nations, that do not

---

[10] www.johnsonplan.com/market-news/insights/insights-2009-07/

make this claim, see us. Did you know that there is a multi-billion dollar industry that is continuously exported from this country? Porn! What does this convey to the world? Is it ok to observe porn and still be a Christian? Isn't this what is being conveyed? What do these scantly clad, female, rock and roll pole dancers convey to the rest of the world as they are on stage twerking, jerking, and strutting their stuff, when once they were conveyed as a role model for young girls? In 2012, $490 billion was spent on entertainment in America.[11] To convey how staggering this amount of money is, if a person made $50,000 a year and spent it all on entertainment, it would take 20 years to spend $1,000,000. It would take 20,000 years to spend $1,000,000,000. It would take 800,000 years to spend $40,000,000,000.

Why are Americans, including many (so-called) committed Christians, so fascinated with Hollywood and what Hollywood produces? It is no wonder there is no fascination with God and that His own people find Him boring. Satan has done a fine job in stealing the hearts and imagination of a whole generation. What God has created and spoken into existence was meant to capture and fascinate. The counterfeiter has created his own wonders to capture men's hearts. God's wonders are seen in trillions of snowflakes of which none are the same. Satan's wonders are trillions of computer generated images that wouldn't even exist if we didn't have electricity. Before I met the Lord, I would contemplate how far you could go out into the universe and end up at the point of no return? Even if you were able to go there and then return, would you ever be the same? We were meant to be continuously fascinated with God, His creation, and seeing Jesus in all His glorious splendor and majestic beauty forever and ever! Most of the world does not see these things. They are looking for something that they call tangible and that can be obtained immediately. Did you know that there are people from all nations that desire to come and live in America

---

[11] http://wallstcheatsheet.com/personal-finance/money-talk-how-does-the-average-american-live.html/?a=viewall;
http://blogs.denverpost.com/fetch/2011/04/10/americans-projected-to-spend-50-84-billion-on-pets-this-year/2962/; http://mentalfloss.com/article/31222/numbers-how-americans-spend-their-money

because of its prosperity and freedom? We have presented to the rest of the world, in our arrogance as a nation, that this is the greatest country to live in (it is and I would not live anywhere else, except for Israel). Yet we have fallen as a Christian nation and are now endeavoring to neutralize this fact by throwing out our "In God we trust" heritage. We have been on this road for a few years. The book of Hosea points out something about Israel that applies to us in America today. In chapter 1:2 it says: *"When the Lord began to speak by Hosea, the Lord said to Hosea: 'Go take yourself a wife of harlotry and children of harlotry, for the land has committed great harlotry by departing from the Lord.'"* As did Israel, so has America. We have departed from the Lord and have committed harlotry. God committed Himself to Israel through the old covenant. God committed Himself, a second time, through the new covenant of the blood of His own Son. If we turn from this and trample His Son and count the blood of the covenant a common thing, will we not be called a great harlot? There were times that I would be tempted to sin and would say in my heart, "I'm going to do this and I'll just ask God to forgive me afterward". God was gracious to always forgive, but in doing this a few times my heart would begin to harden against God. I would sin directly against my own conscience, which is a very dangerous place to be. This very thing is the beginning of a life of compromise and harlotry, if not repented of. Yes, we have fallen from being a Christian nation. We don't want to offend anyone because of religious beliefs. We have had an all out assault against terrorism since 9/11, yet at the same time this country gives more credit to Islam than to Christianity. They have allowed prayer rooms for Islam in many places, but if you pray to Jesus you come under tremendous persecution in this country. The number of Mosques have increased throughout this country and there have even been the shutdown of some streets and areas because of the Muslim call to prayer. We, as a nation, receive all who would come here to live and would not refuse them because of their religious beliefs; yet we are now, as a nation, not wanting to offend anyone. This will be our downfall. I'm reminded of the phrase: "If you don't stand for anything, you will fall for anything!" Is this not what is happening in this country at present? Only a handful are taking a stand for Jesus being "*the way, the truth, and the life*." Many seem to be courting that there are other ways to the Father besides Him.

The Muslim call to prayer is beginning to be heard around the world. Some friends from church spent 3 weeks in Israel. I asked them about what they saw as they were over there. I was shocked by one of the things that they shared. They said that they heard the Muslim call to prayer being broadcast over loud speakers in Jerusalem three times a day![12] Israel is completely surrounded by Muslim nations that hate her and want her completely destroyed. This same "call to prayer" is being broadcasted on the streets of America.[13] America is throwing out Jesus and is opening the floodgates to Islam. Chrislam is growing in America and there has also been the Muslim call to prayer in the church.[14] Just recently on CBN there was an article and video where this happened in a church in Germany.[15] A Christian woman from Germany went to the church were she heard the Muslim call to prayer and stood up calling it an abomination. She was thrown out of the church.

Compare all these things to what Revelation says about the harlot. Again, I ask you, don't take my word for it or reject it without researching it out for yourself! Question everything that I say with the purpose and intent to find out for yourself! The very first verse of the book of Revelation says, *"The Revelation of Jesus Christ, which God gave Him **to show His servants--things which must shortly take place"*** (emphasis mine). First of all you must be one of His servants! What does a servant look like? Jesus exemplified this by washing His disciple's feet. This speaks of cleansing as well as servanthood. He said the one who is already clean needs only to wash his feet. Servanthood keeps us cleansed from the filth of this world as we walk through it. If we are truly one of His servants, He promises that this prophetic word will be opened up to us in understanding through the Spirit's revelation of the Book of Revelation! It would be foolish of us to not pursue understanding

---

[12] https://www.youtube.com/watch?v=c6zzYIsSdHk
[13] https://www.youtube.com/watch?v=ax64N8Bnxyk or https://www.youtube.com/watch?v=oksdM0OOSFo
[14] http://www.eaec.org/bibleanswers/chrislam.htm and https://www.youtube.com/watch?v=ybSAinBMb_g
[15] www.cbn.com/cbnnews/world/2014/February/German-woman-Publicly-Rebuking-Islam-Goes-Viral-/

from Jesus on these things! If you claim His grace, but you're not one of His servants, you are in trouble. The "Day of the Lord" will come as a thief in the night and you will be completely without understanding in those days. Press in to God to be His servant by loving Him. If you have never encountered this Jesus that the Book of Revelation talks about, simply talk to Him and turn from all that you perceive is wickedness and sin. He will embrace you and love you as His own. Blessings.

About the Author:

A nameless lover of Jesus Christ who embraces obscurity. Barely graduating from high school, he went into the highly desired position of limestone wet-saw operator at a stone cutting company, where he met Jesus. He immediately went into obscurity in a Christian community where he lived and worked on staff in the midst of other believers for 20 years. Leaving the community, he then became a "famous" house painter giving his life blood for the next 22 years and raising a family in obscurity. He is now a nameless face still loving Jesus Christ with all his heart. There are many nameless faces throughout the world to which God reveals the intimate mysteries of His heart in the secret place.

I love what Amos answers Amaziah, the priest of Bethel, when he told Amos not to ever prophesy at Bethel again because it was the king's royal sanctuary and residence. Amos humbly answered, *"I was no prophet, nor was I a son of a prophet; but I was a sheepbreeder and a tender of sycamore fruit. Then the Lord took me as I followed the flock and the Lord said to me, 'Go prophesy to My people.'"* He was a nameless lover of God that God raised up in the secret place in order to speak a message to His people!

www.ingramcontent.com/pod-product-compliance
Lightning Source LLC
Chambersburg PA
CBHW060035050426
42448CB00012B/3023